British Contemporary Sculpture at Goodwood 1996-97

Welcome to Sculpture at Goodwood. This is the only venue in Britain where visitors can view an extensive range of current work by major and emerging British sculptors, which has been enabled by the Hat Hill Sculpture Foundation. Over a three year period most of the sculptures will change as we commission more work, replacing those pieces that have been sold. This process has been devised to ensure diversity and encourage the purchase of contemporary British sculpture.

This book features most of the sculptures that are here throughout the 1996-97 season. The sequence of works in the book reflects the order in which you are likely to see them during your walk. On page 98 you will find details of the seating and buildings that are in the copse. These were made by young designers, almost all under the age of twenty-five. If you wish to commission work from them, you may find their details on the Designers and Architect Way Round sheet which is available in the Gallery. Both the Way Round sheet, which lists the sculptures currently on display, and the arrows, designed especially for us by Steven Gregory, are to help you find your way in the copse. Please observe the private areas.

We are grateful to Mr Bryan Robertson for his thoughtful essay *A Home for British Sculpture* which mirrors precisely our own enthusiasm for the work of Britain's sculptors.

Finally, we should like to share with you our pleasure in Sculpture at Goodwood being awarded the National Art Collections Fund Prize 1996 for its outstanding contribution to the enjoyment and awareness of the visual arts. The prize has enabled us to purchase Bill Woodrow's *Sitting on History 1* 1990-95.

Wilfred and Jeannette Cass

A Home for British Sculpture

The presentation of a large number of new or recent sculptures by a broad range of British artists in the open air at Goodwood, an hour's journey from London, is the most important cultural event of the past decade in England. Wilfred and Jeannette Cass, highly individual collectors, have emerged as the custodians of British sculpture in providing it with a beautiful and imaginative setting for the first time. The strategic importance of these ravishing spatial vistas in the almost imperceptibly cultivated natural landscape at Goodwood cannot be exaggerated, not only for the fortunate sculptors but also for collectors, museum and gallery personnel, critics, and those members of the public who want to learn something constructive about the vital art of their own time. Nobody visiting England from abroad concerned with visual art can possibly afford to miss a visit to Goodwood, because only here can you see what is happening in British sculpture now.

Only a small number of commercial galleries in London seriously specialise in contemporary British sculpture, and they have no facilities for housing work which exceeds a certain scale and certainly no place to show it out of doors. Between London and the special exhibitions at the Yorkshire Sculpture Park near Wakefield, there is only - in a more south-westerly direction - the commercial enterprise of Madeleine Ponsonby, in her annual selections of sculpture in the grounds of her Wiltshire home at Roche Court, near Salisbury, but this is a modest affair compared with the big stretch of countryside inhabited by fifty or so sculptures that you find at Goodwood.

Although the imaginative enterprise of Goodwood has been greatly praised and is tremendously appreciated by visitors, I cannot help hoping rather shamefacedly that Goodwood doesn't become too successful. At the Yorkshire Sculpture Park, they're now siting some sculptures in the rough country just outside the artfully landscaped park of Capability Brown with its lake and ponds and smiling lawns.

And already there is talk of constructing a modest roadway and carpark in that rough country just where, to my mind, a carpark should not be. Lavatories will no doubt be clamoured for next, and then a shelter, and then a postcard kiosk, and so it goes. I hope that developments at the excellent Yorkshire Sculpture Park, or blessed lack of them, will prove me wrong. I am merely pointing to the restrictive hazards which, through success, can diminish the character of a place that by definition should ideally be left alone and not tampered with. A plan to erect an 'observation tower' for 'viewing' sculpture within the simple garden and grounds of Henry Moore's home and studios in Hertfordshire was recently and quite sensibly defeated.

Rather differently, the very important outdoor sculpture park at the Kröller-Müller Museum, Otterlo, in Holland has become subtly diminished in the past forty years or so. It is elegantly maintained, but the collection has grown so much that it no longer seems either as special or as physically attractive as it did in the 1950s when Dr Hammacher, one of the great connoisseurs of twentieth-century sculpture, was in charge. A lot of distinctly minimalist sculpture was created internationally in the seventies and early eighties, some of it with refreshing astringency, but the Kröller-Müller seems to have acquired almost too many examples. Some kinds of gallery or studio-bound sculpture don't really require an outdoor setting to achieve their most eloquent presence. There are still marvellous things to see, but in its increased inclusiveness the place seems to have lost its *eclat*. Manufacture has got its foot in the door.

The most beautiful interdependence of sculpture and natural setting that I've ever seen was in the USA, walking around R. Sturgis Ingersoll's sculpture garden at Penllyn, just outside Philadelphia. In addition to serving as chairman of the Philadelphia Museum, Sturgis was a fine collector and the great patron of Jacques Lipchitz in the States, looking after him when he first arrived in America and rebuilding the artist's studio at Hastings-on-the-Hudson when it burned down, with much work destroyed, in an accidental fire. Sturgis owned several powerful Lipchitz bronzes, and Brancusi's *L'Oiselet* as well as Picasso's very moving *Shepherd Holding a Lamb*, placed by some trees in the rolling Pennsylvania countryside which surrounded and seemed a real part of the garden. There were other works, by Matisse, Moore, Laurens and Giacometti among others all looking, in the shadow and sunshine of a summer day, as if they lived there and weren't just on show.

In Connecticut, at his country home, Top Gallant, André Emmerich recently drove me all over the immense acreage of a rolling, densely wooded and spectacular setting for his vast collection of American sculpture, a tonic experience ending in a simple quiet white-painted indoor gallery. And I shall never forget visiting Alexander Calder at Roxburgh, Connecticut, many years ago, and looking at Calder sculptures in the landscape surrounding his studios which confirmed Calder's status as one of the best sculptors for the outdoors that America has produced, in the brilliant company of Isamu Noguchi, David Smith, Alex Lieberman and Mark di Suvero.

In England, the most electrifying counterpoint, so far, between sculpture and setting has been achieved just beyond the formal garden at Kenwood where Moore's *Two Piece Reclining Figure No.5* is placed at the top of a rounded, steep hill with great vistas of Hampstead Heath. Even Moore's critics are won over by this extraordinary spectacle. In the formal garden, you can find Barbara Hepworth's *Monolith (Empyrean)* in blue corrib limestone, which the artist made as a private monument to her elder son, Paul, killed in Korea. It was sited by me, originally, on a terrace facing the river outside the Royal Festival Hall, but the sculpture had to be moved to Kenwood when the building expanded. As a whole we have done very badly by modern sculpture in public places in London. Even the regular temporary displays of sculpture in Battersea Park, initiated by Patricia Strauss, the wife of George Russell Strauss MP, Minister of Supply in the 1945 Labour Government, have ceased, decades ago. Anthony Caro is in my view the most inventive living artist, but visitors to London will search in vain for any works on public view which might justify that statement. The present-day over-crowded Tate Gallery, driven to rotate its collection, might or might not have something on view.

Goodwood is unique in not being 'a sculpture park'. These valuable and often enjoyable places can tame individual sculptures into resembling self-conscious and dumbstruck animals in benign captivity that you stumble across in an open-air menagerie and thus disturb in their semi-slumber. Just as you find yourself in the woods with the dear prancing wallabies, you raise your eyes and there is a menacing rhino on the horizon or, more reassuringly, a shy giraffe. These frivolous thoughts are peculiar to certain experiences in sculpture parks and would not occur to visitors at Goodwood. Here there is no feeling of a park but only the more challenging pleasure of a beautiful, practically untouched, open landscape with variable gradients, woods and copses and some immense vistas of the Sussex countryside beyond. And you discover the sculptures quite slowly, often unexpectedly, in ways that are always to the best advantage of the work. Nothing seems artily sited; everything is beautifully and unselfconsciously placed in an appropriate context.

Most importantly of all, the range of sculpture visible at Goodwood offers us the most broadly based and comprehensive range of work by our younger sculptors that you will find in England. We have always sadly lacked 'educated money' in England, with a dearth of serious collectors for modern art and notably for contemporary sculpture. That is a grave indictment of our fragmented educational system. The

6

majority of our artists, painters or sculptors, are still entirely dependent on foreign sales for survival. But something is stirring, I feel, to have produced Goodwood; and something good in the form of new sources of patronage may develop from our National Lottery extravaganza or with the Millennium projects. In the meantime, let us reflect for a second on the astonishing momentum of sculpture in England that has led to the present rich array of talent presented at Goodwood.

All through my professional life, I've believed that in the stylistically uninfluential but in other ways very productive wake of Henry Moore's example and grand reputation, sculpture in England found a special energy, an incalculable unexpectedness - and nerve, sheer nerve. It's a very long way, after all, in terms of highly original creation, from Jacob Epstein, Henry Moore, Leon Underwood and Barbara Hepworth, Reg Butler, Bernard Meadows, Lynn Chadwick and Kenneth Armitage, through the eccentricities and fantasies of George Fullard, Hubert Dalwood, Bryan Kneale and Michael Sandle, to the architectonic inventions with colour and new synthetic materials in the revolutionary new sculpture of the sixties made by Tim Scott, Phillip King and Anthony Caro - recently honoured in one of the greatest exhibitions of the century in Japan. Beyond Caro, there stretch the highly individual achievements of Nigel Hall, Stephen Cox, Edward Allington, Tony Cragg, Richard Deacon, Andy Goldsworthy, Anish Kapoor, David Nash, Richard Long, Paul Neagu, Alison Wilding and Rachel Whiteread.

What an unparalleled history of imaginative invention! We should honour this history in some concrete way. A survey of sculpture in England from 1900 to the present day opens in Paris this May at the delightful Musée National du Jeu de Paume. But this important show, very near the end of the century, will lack true historical definition in omitting many important figures and key works partly because of space limitations and partly due to the 'conceptual' idea of our sculpture held by the show's distinguished French organiser. It is of national importance for the administrators of the Lottery money to start immediately to plan for the first serious outdoor collection of British sculpture disposed within a new and permanent site in one of the London parks, ideally in Kensington Gardens and Hyde Park, where Moore's noble *Arch* was perfectly sited by the Serpentine, or perhaps Battersea Park with its historic tradition for showing sculpture. It is a serious cultural deprivation, on a national scale, to have nowhere in London where residents and visitors can see a proper spectrum of British sculpture. Our sculpture is, after all, world famous and we should provide a permanent public setting for it. We have great creative genius in England and we should now, at last, face up to our responsibilities in planning for the future, with Goodwood as our inspiration.

Bryan Robertson

Sculpture at Goodwood: the First Year

Spring 1995 saw the opening of the first full season of Sculpture at Goodwood. Two new sculptures were in place, *Requiem* 1986-95 by Ana Maria Pacheco and *Granite Catamarans on a Granite Wave* 1994 by Stephen Cox. Both were enabled by the Hat Hill Sculpture Foundation, and both were pieces already worked on by the artists, and completed with the Foundation's help. The realisation of these pieces heralded new ways for artists and Sculpture at Goodwood to work together.

In its pursuit of excellence in sculpture and to demonstrate a diversity of medium, this year Sculpture at Goodwood invited Vong Phaophanit to show a work made in neon. In *Azure Neon Body* 1994-95, a long trench, filled at random with Laotian script fashioned in azure neon light, glows beneath an avenue of trees. The energy emerging from the earth through this jumble of text nestling against the chalk is undeniable and adds to the ever-extending range of what sculpture can be.

Significant loans have also been added to the collection at Sculpture at Goodwood through the year, older works by major artists, which deserve to be seen by a wider public. Richard Long's *Six Stone Circles* 1981 in Delabole slate has been loaned to Sculpture at Goodwood for three years. It is placed, as the artist desired, in a circle of trees: a spot for reflection and calm. Made especially to be seen in the open air, the stone circles merge with the earth, quietly yet assertively. Two pieces by Phillip King, *Slant* 1966 and *Genghis Khan* 1963, were loaned from separate sources. King's *Academy Piece* 1971, which was here for the opening, will be replaced by a new work made especially for Sculpture at Goodwood. John Maine's Portland stone *Enclosure* 1995 arrived in August this year, the year in which he was made Royal Academician, and it sits well within the lawn at the entrance to Sculpture at Goodwood. Peter Randall-Page has kindly arranged the loan of *Secret Life I and IV* 1994, both carved in Finnish granite boulders. These replace *Ways to Wrap a Stone I and II* 1990 and *Beneath the Skin* 1991. Sculpture at Goodwood has entered into a partnership with the BOC Group to restore Richard Deacon's *When the Landmasses First Appeared* 1986, which is in their collection of contemporary art at the BOC headquarters in Windlesham, Surrey. Before the sculpture is returned to its normal site, it will be displayed at Sculpture at Goodwood for two years. This demonstrates yet another way in which Sculpture at Goodwood can work with artists and other collections.

Sculpture on Saturdays was the Foundation's main educational activity during 1995. This series of study days organised in collaboration with West Dean College (The Edward James Foundation) was launched in April with Eilís O'Connell and Laurence Bradbury. The day focused on O'Connell's sculpture. A visit to Hat Hill and her exhibition of new sculpture in the Gallery at Sculpture at Goodwood was followed by supper and a lecture by Laurence Bradbury at West Dean. Visitors were able to get closer to the sculpture through direct contact with the artist and by listening to and joining in with the conversation between the artist and the art historian. New pieces made especially for the exhibition showed O'Connell's continued fascination with weaving metal, first manifest in *Space Emptied Out* 1994 which was commissioned for the opening of Sculpture at Goodwood. New forms and the introduction of colour in *Collar Creel* 1995 showed that she was moving forward quickly, and her thirst for new materials was evident. Abundant bluebells in the copse outside the gallery gave an excellent background to a large woven steel creel (basket).

Through the year the copse with its new planting has matured, enveloping spaces for sculpture and making them more like 'galleries' for single pieces, as was originally envisaged. When the sun is high in summertime, light floods into these galleries from above, but when the sun is lower in the sky in spring, autumn and winter, the slanting light through the trees, in varying degrees of leaf, changes the view of sculpture dramatically. The colour of the sun also alters the surface of the work, as does its intensity in differing weather conditions or times of day and season.

An artist who has harnessed nature in its fullest sense within his work is Andy Goldsworthy. In a new commission at Hat Hill in June 1995, he not only used Sussex chalk and wood from the copse in his sculptures but also the time of day and moonlight. In *A Clearing of Arches. For the Night* 1995, a group of dry-stone chalk arches, made secure with flakes of flint and placed at random in a rough clearing at the edge of the copse, he used the light of the moon on the chalk to set the work aglow. His photographs, which will eventually be the only evidence that the sculpture existed, are works of art in their own right.

Andy Goldsworthy's study day was a highlight of the year, and the conversation between the artist and Professor Norbert Lynton was memorable - even more for being able to see the chalk arches in the fading summer twilight, appearing to become lighter as the day darkened. A chalk line which snaked through the Gallery at Sculpture at Goodwood and beyond, a chalk ring with an inner circle of chalk burnished with flint, a dome of twigs gathered from the copse surrounding a large 'snowball' of chalk, and two drawings, contrasting rubbings, one in chalk the other in graphite, completed the accompanying exhibition.

The third study day featured Ana Maria Pacheco who, with David Elliott, Director of the Museum of Modern Art in Oxford, opened up her world of strange and wondering travellers to the audience. Ana Maria Pacheco's sculpture conceals a wealth of meaning beneath the beautifully carved and coloured surfaces, and carefully considered and answered questions revealed the route to understanding and greater appreciation. The Gallery, peopled with the figures of Pacheco's installation *Man and his Sheep* 1989, was proved to be flexible and sympathetic to showing diverse work, and the programme for 1996 will continue to test it.

Sculpture on Saturdays 1996 will have a slightly altered form. The three days, featuring Stephen Cox with David Cohen (11 May), Edward Allington with Cathy de Monchaux (29 June) and Nigel Hall with William Packer (5 October), will be based entirely at Sculpture at Goodwood. Beginning at 11.00 am with a walk around the copse and conversation with the artist and critic about the major work that the artist has on display, the day will continue with lunch and then a lecture/forum in the Gallery at Sculpture at Goodwood, ending at around 4.00 pm. This altered timetable is an experiment intended to find out the kind of composition our visitors prefer. For participants who wish to make a weekend in Chichester, the option of staying at West Dean will still be open, provided space is available.

Planning for further educational activity with schools and colleges in West Sussex has taken place in the course of 1995, with the result that an Education Pack has been published. Felicity Allen, an expert in gallery education, has advised Sculpture at Goodwood on the content, and the pack will be available for teachers planning visits throughout this season. This is a lively document, not only giving pointers with regard to the National Curriculum at all key stages but also geared towards helping everyone to look at sculpture, to understand and enjoy it much more thoroughly.

New sculpture regularly replaces pieces which have been sold. Peter Logan's *Duet for Two Flutes* 1991, Elisabeth Frink's *Horse and Rider* 1969, two sets of Steven Gregory's *Bag Men* 1993,

Andy Goldsworthy's *A Clearing of Arches. For the Night* 1995,
Robin Connelly's *Oak Spiral* 1991 and *The Kiss* 1991 by George Cutts
have all been sold in the course of 1995. New sculptures for 1996
include new works by Anthony Caro, Zadok Ben-David, Peter Burke,
Lynn Chadwick, Laura Ford, Steven Gregory, Charles Hadcock,
Allen Jones, Bryan Kneale, David Mach, Cathy de Monchaux,
Michael Sandle and Bill Woodrow. During the course of the year other
artists will be working on proposals for Sculpture at Goodwood, as
the aim is to introduce about one new piece a month into the display
whilst selling or removing another.

A team of volunteer guides plays a very important role at Sculpture
at Goodwood. The guides are kept regularly informed about new work
and changes. They welcome visitors and are willing to accompany
people on their walk in the grounds and talk about the sculptures
should visitors wish. More volunteers are needed, and applications
are welcomed from people passionate about sculpture and interested
in meeting people. Some guides are being trained to become research
assistants and help with the growing volume of work at Sculpture at
Goodwood.

Sculpture at Goodwood has travelled with the artists who have worked
with the Foundation throughout the year, and the resulting sculptures
and events have given much pleasure to visitors.

Ann Elliott, Head of Sculpture

Glynn Williams
Gateway of Hands 1992
bronze, H 335 cm
Enabled by the Hat Hill Sculpture Foundation

This is Glynn Williams's largest sculpture to date, of which there are two casts in bronze. This, the original, welcomes visitors to Sculpture at Goodwood.

The piece is typical of Williams's work, demonstrating his unique blend of figuration and abstraction. He first employed the notion of slicing into naturalistic forms and shifting the pieces into new relationships in *Portrait with Flowers* 1990-91, which was shown at Sculpture at Goodwood during the first season. The dynamism which he found this method of working gave to the forms can be seen in the hands, which from the front look quite realistic, but from behind take on a curious ambiguity. With the hands, the implied movement of opening the palm in a gesture of welcome is underlined by the centre sections of each hand being sliced and swivelled, out in one, slightly inward in the other; pushed forward in one and slightly back in the other. The way in which the hands interact is also curious. Having been parted in the gesture of greeting, they are sited as two separate elements, but the composition remains as one, largely through the continuation of strong diagonals in each which are readily linked by the eye.

Such compositional devices were used by the cubists in their quest for a better understanding of form. In Picasso's *Glass of Absinthe*, he moved portions of the glass and its contents into new relationships to give a whole view: an entire experience of seeing round and within the form. So it is with these hands.

The hands are a self-portrait, undeniably those of their maker.

Phillip King
Genghis Khan 1963
plastic, H 213 cm
Private Collection

Genghis Khan is one of six sculptures made by King in the early 1960s devoted to the cone form. The first, *Rosebud*, has a delicate pink plastic shell, cut to reveal an inner form which is dark green. *Twilight* followed, and is perhaps the most complex of the six: the outer portion of half the cone is cut into ribbons and, whilst still attached at the apex, these are formed into a horizontal plane. The third is *Genghis Khan*, a dark purple threatening presence, with shapes creeping out from beneath the cone enclosure. The shapes themselves appear similar to those that were cut in *Twilight*, but put together in a different arrangement. Two such pieces are attached to the apex and sides of the cone as great wings. On first examination they appear to be the same, but the cuts are entirely different in detail.

Tim Hilton in his book *The Sculpture of Phillip King* (Henry Moore Foundation/Lund Humphries 1992) writes: '*Genghis Khan* seems to be clothed rather than stripped. Its fantasy may allude to strange natural forces, water spilling in ravines in remote mountains: hence the allusion to Coleridge's poem. There is also the temptation to call this one of King's most North African subjects, or to think of it in terms of Islamic architecture.'

The cones are perhaps also slightly surrealist in nature, a quality which emerges at different times in King's oeuvre, for example in *Cross Over* 1979 and *Frankfurt Maquette* 1989-90.

Bruce Gernand
Hearts-Hide 1993
bronze, H 148 cm
The Artist

From 1992 to 1994 Bruce Gernand was Henry Moore Fellow in Sculpture at Central St Martin's College of Art and Design. He worked in the college foundry, and the largest sculpture he made there was *Hearts-Hide*.

Bronze sculptures, unless very small, are cast in sections and welded together. Normally these sections form a 'skin' which, when conjoined, give shape and volume to the whole. *Hearts-Hide* celebrates this process by revealing in its own form every aspect of its construction.

Bruce Gernand, in his catalogue for his exhibition at the end of the Fellowship, writes: 'Large bronze sculptures tend to be read as a mass, giving an undeniable impression of solidity... In making *Hearts-Hide*, one of my intentions was to expose these features of production. Taking the notion of segments to an extreme, I cast an excessive 27 pieces which are assembled like a jigsaw puzzle with the majority of the joining left exposed. In fact, flanges, brackets, gaps and welds become integral to the work revealing the process of its making and emphasising the surfaces worked and having undergone transformations. Whilst there is clearly a lot of metal in the object - because of its open form, apertures, piercing and segmentation - its "monumental" references are suspended by features of fragmentation and fragile thinness of skin.'

This is indeed a vulnerable image, slightly animal in character, but not intentionally so. Through his direct involvement in the casting process, Gernand has sought to understand it fully. Material and process have become the subject of the work itself.

Ian Hamilton Finlay
The World Has Been Empty Since the Romans 1985
Bath stone, steel chain, L 735 cm
Victoria Miro, London

These slabs of stone, resembling fragments from a Roman
archaeological site, with their carefully inscribed words in classical
letter-form, are a very bleak statement. Made in collaboration with
a stone mason, the poem sets up trails of thoughts about European
culture. But is this rhetoric? Is it a metaphor? Finlay proposes the right
sentiment through the most appropriate medium, and we believe that
at Hat Hill, close to evidence of Roman occupation, the sculpture has
found its most fitting place.

THE WORLD·HAS·BEEN·EMPTY·SINCE·THE·ROMANS

Edward Allington
Fallen Pediment (Piano) 1994
copper, L 300 cm
Enabled by the Hat Hill Sculpture Foundation

This is the only sculpture, so far, that Edward Allington has made to be shown in the open air. He was persuaded to do so by the qualities of light and colour that Hat Hill Copse had to offer, when towards the end of the day on his first visit to the copse the light falling through the trees shed a red glow over the green ground cover and the trees appeared to be as perfect as those in a Japanese garden. His choice of copper for the sculpture is reflected in his first impressions, although it is a metal that he loves and uses frequently.

Elements of architecture and the realm of classicism which are central to Allington's work are here in *Fallen Pediment*, the concept for which at first seemed to be relatively simple. He planned to make a form which appeared to be resting lightly on the ground, with a modest presence that you might miss should you not be looking carefully. When he began to draw the slightly roofed pediment shape, distorted by pulling it round in a horizontal plane, he thought that the resolution would be straightforward. 'I started to try to draw it and although I could make quite reasonable freehand sketches of the way I thought it might be, drawing in a technical manner always failed. I presumed my technical draughtsmanship was not up to it, so I did not worry about it.' However, when he began to work with sheet metalworkers they all began to realise how problematical the construction was going to be. He also made a cardboard structure which failed in the same way as the drawings, but slowly the work was resolved, revealing in the process the tricks that stonemasons employ when carving pediments for buildings.

David Nash
Charred Column 1993
burnt oak, H 510 cm
Annely Juda Fine Art, London

A totem, but furthermore a structure reminiscent of Brancusi's *Endless Column* 1936/37, placed at the end of The Avenue of Heroes in Tirgu-Jiu, Romania, *Charred Column* finds its own place between these extremes of verticality.

This is one of a series of columns made by David Nash in a variety of woods, the first in 1983 in sycamore, at the Forest Park in St Louis, now in a collection in Florida. One was destroyed in a gallery fire in Chicago, another was made in Japan in 1984 and is now in the collection of Setagya Museum. The first oak column was made in Belgium and is now in a private collection in the south of France.

Charred Column, the next to be made in oak, was started in 1991 at David Nash's studio, Capel Rhiw, in Blaenau Ffestiniog. He has used only the heartwood of the oak trunk for this sculpture, the sap wood having been cut away. V-shaped cuts were made in the column to create the divisions within the form and then the whole was rolled into fire, a portion at a time, in order to burn the wood to its final shape and colour.

The carbon surface almost denies the natural qualities of the wood, and allows the viewer to think more of the form than of the material from which the sculpture is made. The velvet black of *Charred Column* affords a vivid contrast with living trees in all seasons. In summer it hides mysteriously in the shaded canopy, in spring it glows against the pale green of the beech, and in winter it stands in full light against the grey trunks of the surrounding trees, in stark contrast with frost or snow.

Avril Wilson
A Leaf with Halo 1991
steel, L 100 cm
Private Collection

The skeleton leaf wrought in steel that has been curled and welded sits on a decaying tree stump amongst real fallen leaves. The 'halo', made from similar elements but with a slightly different construction, is positioned on another part of the stump, and is akin to a fungal growth, the sort of growth that is nourished by decaying vegetation. Within this simple arrangement there lies the full circle of life.

Avril Wilson is a blacksmith. Much of her work is functional, but at the same time extremely decorative and sometimes almost medieval in character. *A Leaf with Halo* is a little different from the complex foliage and the other natural forms which lie at the heart of her craft, because of the simplicity of its structure. Trees, leaves, pods, fruits, shells, suns and moons are wrought from metal and assembled, finding form in objects as diverse as candle holders, gates and decorative arches.

A Leaf with Halo quickly asserts its presence on the woodland floor, entirely at home amongst the beauty that inspired it.

Elisabeth Frink
Riace Figures II, III, IV 1987, 1988, 1989
bronze, H 189.2 cm, 189.2 cm, 191.4 cm
The Estate of Elisabeth Frink

These tall imposing figures were inspired by two fifth-century Greek statues of warriors found in the sea off Calabria, southern Italy, in the 1970s. Frink is known for her preference for the male figure over that of the female. She also had a tendency to work in series, and in these figures she brings together her preference and her inclination. The *Riace* figures are typical of her mature work, and her technical excellence shows through this subject-matter. The models from which her figures were cast were made in plaster, a material introduced to her by Bernard Meadows when he was teaching at Chelsea School of Art. Plaster built up round a metal aperture can be modelled and carved as well as used to support other materials. Frink's great sensitivity to surface is seen in these figures through this working method; the face of one of the group shows quite clearly where scrim had been applied to the surface before it was cast in bronze.

'The original figures,' writes Frink, 'were very beautiful, but also very sinister, and that is what they are supposed to be. ... these were warriors who would go out and fight your battles for you, mercenaries, but in return they had to have certain sacrifices made to them. In other words they were thugs. Even though I don't particularly like sinister things, thuggishness is a bit of a preoccupation with me. It all hinges on my humanitarian sentiments.' Quoted from Frink: *A Portrait*, written with Edward Lucie-Smith and published by Bloomsbury in 1994, after her death.

Frink's fascination with the fact that these figures had two sides to them is brought out in her set of *Riace* figures. She has used different coloured patinas to put masks on them. 'It's a way of showing that their beauty in a sense hides what they are up to.'

Steven Gregory
Paparazzi 1996
bronze, H 152.4 cm
Enabled by the Hat Hill Sculpture Foundation

Groups are seldom benign, whether massed people, flocks of birds or herds of animals - there is always an element of unease and unpredictability about them. As with his very successful series, *Bag Men* 1993, which were featured in *Sculpture at Goodwood 1*, this parade of anthropomorphic cameras gives rise to feelings of revulsion, horror and humour. The cameras on vultures' legs tell us that they prey on their victims - such images surely inhabit the nightmares of most members of the glitterati. The menacing stance of these creatures, their undeniably black patina giving character to their black souls, is intensified by their group presence. Hunting in a pack, they survive, but ultimately this is the survival of the fittest as they seemingly jostle for position to get the best shot.

Gregory collected ancient stills cameras and a movie camera, finding them in antique markets and second-hand shops, and used them to create different characters within this group. Their individuality is emphasised in different ways: the bellows in one, the placing of the camera vertically or horizontally in others. After all, we are all unique. The smallest of these dark beings sneaks to the fore to gain a better view, the extended claw of one towards the rear menaces both his colleagues and their prey. The glistening eyes of the lenses, their penetrating collective eye, serve to emphasise their intent, and are a subtle but essential touch in this assembly.

Is this a severe case of media bashing? Possibly. More likely a wry look at a phenomenon of the late twentieth century, a marked sign of our times.

Laura Ford
Nature Girls 1996
bronze, H 110 cm
Enabled by the Hat Hill Sculpture Foundation

Laura Ford has been thinking about how sculpture operates within a landscape and wanted to make something that would become part of it, but which on closer observation would be rather strange in that environment. She started with the *Stump Girl*, which takes the form of a regular tree stump animated by a pair of little girls' legs. The later *Conifer Girl* and *Bush Girl* which complete this unruly trilogy, add to the conundrum. When brought together they give rise to questions of identity, intent, fear and humour. Are these depictions of real trees? Are they watching? Are they malevolent? They provoke parental concern, but remain beyond our reach. The sculptures are made in a traditional material, bronze, with all its authority and associations with important monuments. It is employed here to suggest a different scenario. The artist has used the convention of perfect outdoor sculpture for a subversive subject-matter.

The *Conifer* and *Bush* are quieter than their *Stump* counterpart, but possibly more malevolent. Simultaneously they have the innocent joy of girls playing in the wood and the bleakness of children gone missing. In a gallery setting (they were first shown at Spacex in Exeter in an exhibition for which they were especially cast by Sculpture at Goodwood) they are hopelessly attempting to camouflage themselves, like children hiding their heads and thinking they cannot be seen. A landscape setting such as this renders their fantasy almost a reality. *Nature Girls* are uneasy, but comical. Laura Ford shares with Camille Paglia a view of nature which, like sexuality, is at times romanticised but is brutal and cruel. *Nature Girls* evolved from a series of works devoted to the tyranny and contradictions manifest in children. All of these girls are egotistical, attention-seeking and aggressive as well as possessing the opposite qualities.

Bernard Meadows

Large Seated Armed Figure 1963
bronze, H 75 cm
Private Collection

Large Seated Armed Figure is a classic example of Bernard Meadows's
work, in subject matter, in the tensions exhibited within the forms and
the contrasts between them. It is a confrontational piece, at once
aggressive and vulnerable. The blades of knives and spears jut from the
sides of the figure which appears to be clothed in a flack jacket. However, the figure is naked but for this slight cover, and his unprotected
human attributes leave him as vulnerable as the rest of us. Meadows
made other sculptures close in form to this, standing, sitting and armed,
first in plaster then cast in bronze.

Another cast of this sculpture belongs to the Keatley Trust and is on
loan to the Fitzwilliam Museum, Cambridge.

Other preoccupations throughout Meadows's career have been crab
and bird forms, and he has kept largely to these references, and to the
human figure, in his sculpture, drawing and collage, however abstract
the work might be. These armed figures came a few years before
Meadows began working with softer rounded forms, erotic imagery
in highly polished bronze, which contrast greatly with the awkwardly
composed crabs and cockerels, jabbing and squawking.

Andy Goldsworthy
Herd of Arches 1994
sandstone and slate, L 1500 cm (approx)
Michael Hue-Williams, London

The quarry at Gatelawbridge in Dumfriesshire was the site of a work which is illustrated in *Stone* by Andy Goldsworthy (Viking/Penguin Books, 1994) under the inscription:

> Out of the quarry
> seven arches
> made over two days
> no failures
> one almost fell -
> slipped down the face of a rock
> as I removed supporting stones

This was the first manifestation of the sandstone arches, made entirely in the spirit of Goldsworthy's practice of using materials in their place of origin. The stone from this quarry was used in the construction of major eighteenth- and nineteenth-century buildings which make up much of Glasgow, the distinct pink colour lending warmth to the northern townscape.

This notion of movement found its way into *Herd of Arches*, a group which seems to have wandered in search of a new location. Sited by Andy Goldsworthy and Joe Smith at Hat Hill Copse, the *Arches* are placed along a pathway winding between fairly dense trees, against a dark green ground-cover of ivy. Here the colour contrast between the red stone and the green ground lends a strong dynamic to the piece, which first emerged against its own colour in the rough waste ground of the quarry.

Andy Goldsworthy

A Clearing of Arches. For the Night 1995
Sussex chalk, flint, H 120 cm (approx)
Enabled by the Hat Hill Sculpture Foundation

In 1994 when Andy Goldsworthy was working on the installation of
Herd of Arches at Hat Hill, he began to play with the chalk and flint
that he found in the copse. He covered leaves with powdered chalk,
and made leaf prints in chalk scraped from around the flints which
traced walks along the woodland paths. These were soon washed
away by the rain, but it was obvious that he was captivated by the
material. Remembering that chalk was used to mark paths for walks
at night, and because the sandstone arches were already marking a
path through the copse, Goldsworthy was led to the idea of making
arches for a particular time of day, in this case for the night.

When he was discussing the Hat Hill project, how to do it and the tools
to use, images of the Arctic, where he had made earlier arch forms in
snow and ice, kept coming back to him. 'When I was in the Arctic I
wrote in my diary something like, "I keep on talking about the snow
and ice as a landscape because it feels as solid as if it is the earth," but
in fact it was water and that made me realise the movement in stone.
When I returned from the Arctic I made a stone arch as an echo of the
one I made in the North Pole and now I find the white stone, it is very
interesting.'

The more Goldsworthy became involved with the chalk arches, the
more he became aware of their significance. 'It is like the keystone in
the arch that slots into place, it's the same with the ideas. You build up
these things and suddenly the thing is complete and this is another
arch. The idea is part of a bigger arch, if you like, of which the pieces
are spread all over the place.'

Paul Neagu
Triple Starhead 1987-93
stainless steel, H 500 cm
Enabled by the Hat Hill Sculpture Foundation

For Paul Neagu sculpture is a catalyst for ideas and their social role. His works are archetypes for notions that are not normally seen in concrete form. In *Triple Starhead* he has taken the opened up shape of a shooting star and constructed it in three repeated forms firmly bolted together and rooted in the ground. However, the soaring head with its 'comet's tail' conveys meanings quite contrary to those of a heavy earthbound object. The convention of a blurred photographic image capturing a moving body is relevant here, and the 'tail', a graphic device used by cartoonists, acts as a visual thrust whilst in fact being an anchor. The shimmering surface of stainless steel worked to swirling textures endows the material with additional resonance in both sunlight and moonlight, heightening the concepts behind *Triple Starhead*.

David Mach
The Garden Urn 1996
galvanised wire coat hangers, H 250 cm
Enabled by the Hat Hill Sculpture Foundation

David Mach employs no end of curious and unrelated materials and man-made objects in his sculpture. From piles of unused newspapers and magazines he has fashioned full-scale classical columns; from rubber tyres, submarines and Greek temples; from match heads, the most colourful portraits, and from burnt match heads, sombre ones. It is from the match heads that a series of portraits using wire coat hangers emerged. The sitter's face was modelled, and the contours described with closely assembled rows of hangers the hooks providing a shimmering aura around the head.

This *Garden Urn* came about because David Mach was interested in the over-decorated, reproduction garden urns that can be found in garden centres. Given Mach's long fascination with kitsch items, this was not unusual, but the twist in the tale came when Sculpture at Goodwood asked him for one of his wire coat hanger garden urns. He had not made one, but thought this to be a reasonable idea for a sculpture. We found that the gardens of Biddulph Grange, a National Trust property in Staffordshire, had the ideal sugar-bowl urn. With the help of the head gardener, Bill Maleclei, photographs were taken and the shape and scale approved by Mach. The National Trust's Mercia Regional Office gave permission for Mach's assistant, Philip Stroud, to take a copy of the urn, which he made in fibreglass. The sculpture will be completed when David Mach has filled it to overflowing with fruits, opulent and extravagant. The coat hangers were laboriously assembled on to the urn by Adrian Moakes at his workshops in Manchester. The result is a sculpture of enormous humour and curious beauty, resplendent in a sylvan setting, which cocks a snook at our preconceptions and desires for the status that such objects are supposed to imply.

Vong Phaophanit

Azure Neon Body 1994-1995
neon lights, perspex, L 700 cm
The Artist

Some time ago Vong Phaophanit came across a small book, a dictionary translating Laotian into English. Published by a Laotian prince in the 1970s, the book also contained essays about Laotian life, and that of the prince in particular. Some words, for example 'please ' and 'thank you', were not included. However, a whole section was devoted to words describing the human body - skin, hair, leg, sweat, liver, kidneys, fingernails and so on, and these provide the basis, in Laotian script, for *Azure Neon Body*.

One hundred and seventy-two words, piled randomly in a trench in the ground, emanate a strong azure light: energy from the earth seeming to celebrate the energy of mankind.

This sculpture was first shown, in a smaller version, in the exhibition *Cocido y Crudo* (Cooked and Raw), 14 December 1994 - 6 March 1995 at the Reina Sofia Gallery in Madrid. In the gallery it was set into a false floor and flooded the room with bright blue light. In its woodland setting the sculpture has to compete with natural light. This brings a new dimension to *Azure Neon Body*, one of time, day or season, which in the copse is accompanied by the vagaries of changing light, shadow and weather.

Vong Phaophanit has used the little book as the basis for other sculpture: its curious, almost crude quality kindles ideas not remotely thought of by its publisher.

Phillip King
Slant 1966
arborite, painted, L 457 cm
The Artist

Phillip King made *Slant* shortly after *Slit*, both similar arrangements of flat surfaces and both a development of the cone idea, manifest in *Rosebud* and *Genghis Khan*. The principles of 'standing up' were a preoccupation at the time, as was the idea of 'leaning', exemplified in *Span* and *Brake*, also made in 1966.

It is quite easy to see how *Slant* develops from the idea of planks leaning together, perhaps less easy to see how the shapes are arrived at from a cone. In developing his idea from *Slit*, Phillip King took a sheet of card, bent it, drew chevrons on it and then twisted it to arrive at the point where the form could be broken. The cut shapes were then assembled by sitting one on top of another. Flattened, the six elements could be reassembled into one open sheet with a bend in the middle.

Slant was first painted green for an exhibition at the Rowan Gallery in Bruton Place in 1966. However, he changed the colour to red for an exhibition in Battersea Park, as he was worried about showing the green sculpture against grass. It has remained red ever since.

Phillip King came across arborite, the material from which *Slant* is constructed, when he was investigating plastics. It is like formica in substance, a hard plastic that can be machine cut and which is extremely durable. Arborite was manufactured in different colours, but not liking these, King painted the surface in matt eggshell paint, applied with a roller, to saturate the piece in strong colour. Soaking the atmosphere with colour gave resonance to the sculpture and suggests dancing and flowers opening.

Charles Hadcock
Caesura IV 1995
cast iron, H 500 cm
Enabled by the Hat Hill Sculpture Foundation

Caesura: a pause near the middle of a line, or a break between words within a metrical foot, specifically in Greek and Latin poetry. *Caesura* for Charles Hadcock is a series of sculptures in which he explores and celebrates fragmentation, mathematics, multiplicity and the impossible. In *Caesura IV* the two fragments of a single sphere are turned against each other, making it impossible for the globe to be completed. It seems that if the eye were to carry the ascending curves to their conclusion, they would first form an arch, and then complete their circle under the earth. Furthermore, the blocks which form *Caesura IV* are all identical, apart from those at the edges where there are no bolt holes. Their placement suggests that they would complete a globe, but the fact that they do not diminish in size towards the poles makes this impossible. These twists in function are enjoyed by the artist as he alters the mathematics of the form, releases the geometry and then destroys the apparent function.

The plates of cast iron, bolted together with industrial precision, are made to the rules of the Golden Section (the division of a line so that the whole is to the greater as that part is to the smaller part), and in this case are based on the proportions of the artist's body. The outer skin is turned inwards showing the 'industrial' construction of multiple parts, thus turning on its head the logic with which the composition was formed. The textured surface is a celebration of man-made replicas of natural forms, as Charles Hadcock prefers to delve into areas first explored by others, the challenge posed by nature seeming too great. His abiding interest in mathematics, architecture, archaeology, the recent industrial past and manufacturing processes testifies to this.

Shirazeh Houshiary
The Extended Shadow 1994
lead, gold leaf, H 400 cm
Enabled by the Hat Hill Sculpture Foundation

Shirazeh Houshiary's early ambition was to be a writer, and of *The Extended Shadow* she has written: 'The "Heptad" or group of seven was called by Greek philosophers "Minerva" because of its similarity to the goddess in fables, ie it is virgin and unmarried, neither is born from mother (even number) or father (odd number). One could say that heptad proceeds from the "monad" (number one) which is the summit of numbers because it is indivisible by both odd and even numbers. The monad symbolised intellect, male/female and God for the Pythagoreans. Heptad alliance to the monad has made it sacred in many traditions.

The Extended Shadow is a column of four metres in height and constructed of a series of seven sided polygons, ie heptagons, stacked upon each other. These are made of cast lead with the top and underside finished in gold.

'The squaring of the number seven (symbolised by the heptagon) is realised by repeating heptagon forty-nine times in its vertical dimension. Each turns around its centre as they ascend, until a full circle is completed. This act of rotation reveals the inner core of gold and the movement of seven gold lines spiralling upwards around the column. Now one sees the column of density and weight slowly turning to subtleness and light. This process of change is the true meaning of *The Extended Shadow*.'

Bill Woodrow

*Endeavour: Cannon Dredged from the
First Wreck of the Ship of Fools* 1994
bronze, L 440 cm
Enabled by the Hat Hill Sculpture Foundation

> The world of fools has such a store,
> That he who would not see an ass
> Must bide at home and bolt his door,
> And break his looking glass. Anon

This is the tenth sculpture in a series devoted to the theme of the 'Ship of Fools', a commentary on the foolishness of mankind wrapped in wry humour. Uncomfortably penetrating insights into human frailty and our seeming inability to learn from experience are all present in *Endeavour*. At first sight the bronze cannon looks real and convincing, a traditional weapon of war with its terrible ammunition placed in a pile close by and ready for use. On closer inspection, however, the image falls apart. The cannon balls are representations of our world. The gun-barrel is the trunk of a tree, sprouting a leafy growth; it is supported by a crouching 'stick' man, sexually well endowed. Potential movement is found to be impossible as the wheels could not possibly work. They are metaphors for aspects of human life. Books represent an accumulation of knowledge from which we seem not to learn and here become dubious supports. A reel of cord, staked to the ground so that forward motion would cause it to unwind, hints at futility. A drum, the skin of which is pierced so that it could not possibly be played, is supported by a spindle which is a burning candle and would soon cease to exist. The last, a tray of food to keep the prisoner alive, has a spindle which is a flute for music to feed the mind. A prisoner? Well, yes, the undercarriage appears to be a prison door. Music sustains us, the prisoner plays a rousing tune on his accordion, the wolf/dog (the head of the man/man's friend?) bites its own leg.

Tony Cragg
Trilobites 1989
bronze, H 200 cm
Private loan

'Sometimes pictures are puzzled together. For example, Darwin's theories and a mass of geological studies have together led to visualisations of trilobite-infested primeval seas and vast tropical forests, dinosaurs, mammoths, and last but not least, man.' Tony Cragg
Artforum March 1988

In *Trilobites* Tony Cragg has taken two motifs, that of the three-lobed body of a marine fossil of Palaeozoic times and a vessel from the laboratory. Neither reference is strange in his work, but the unseen notions that pull this piece together and make it appear as it does are many and varied. Cragg uses a plethora of materials and references for his sculpture, reduced here to a pair of simple primordial forms, but with a wider message. In their original state, trilobites may be around 4 cm in length; here we see them as if under the microscope. They have been enlarged, all the better for you to see the form and understand it. But Cragg's sculpture is not straightforward, there is also an underlying threat of unease. The laboratory vessels, set into the surfaces, spoil the simple enlargement, as if a horrible disease has infested the simple creatures. Might it therefore be possible to find here a metaphor for evolution in several ways? The natural, the engineered, or the accidental?

Whichever way we allow our thoughts to wander around the issues addressed in this sculpture, and the possibilities it offers, it is perhaps essential to remember that Cragg is not dogmatic, but is helping us to see more, more clearly.

Eva Drewett
The Human Side of Being II 1991
bronze, H 400 cm
Private Collection

Eva Drewett writes: 'The human persona changes according to how we are treated by others. Our character is constantly changing depending on whom we are reacting to. We naturally react to impulses evoked by others. Our behavioural patterns are forever altering like a kaleidoscope. This piece focuses on just one image of that kaleidoscope. The exterior is human but asexual - the back has been distorted slightly so that it is impossible to determine sex. The interior is symbolic of one image of our kaleidoscopic nature'.

The Human Side of Being has been made in three versions: a smaller piece in an edition of eight in bronze; *The Human Side of Being II*, an edition of four monumental bronzes, the first of which is on display at Hat Hill Copse; and another version made in ceramic which Eva Drewett says she completed after several failures, having wanted to make the work in a medium other than bronze. The textures of the inner and outer surfaces provide contrasts similar to those in the bronze versions.

Richard Long
Six Stone Circles 1981
Delabole slate, D 375 cm
Private Collection

In the 1960s, Richard Long made one of the most significant break-
throughs in the development of British sculpture when he chose to
explore the realms of distance and space in a particular way. Not
unusual concerns for a sculptor, but the scale of his work, and the
way it is recorded, gave new dimensions to sculptural practice. He
undertook marathon walks in the most distant and deserted places in
the world, and made sculptures relating to those landscapes.
A particular part of a terrain would be singled out and a composition
involving that view would be made with objects found on the site.
Recorded as photographs, maps and short texts, these works have
evolved throughout his career. He also collects materials which he
brings in to the gallery or museum, local materials, possibly, materials
that are relevant to the place, and arranges simple circles, rectangles,
squares or lines in response to the architecture of the building. His
highly developed sense of space ensures a completely satisfying and
'correct' placement and alignment: stones, sticks, lumps of coal, slate,
chalk or flint, variously positioned in solid or linear forms.

Six Stone Circles is a slightly different work. Normally Long's outdoor
sculpture is ephemeral, useful only until it is recorded, then left for
nature to do her worst. Here is a permanent piece sited in an outdoor
setting. The Delabole slate from a quarry in Cornwall is arranged in six
concentric circles, the larger pieces in the outer circle, the smaller ones
at the centre. This sculpture was originally commissioned by Mrs Kieler,
on the advice of Dr David Brown when he was a Curator of the Modern
Collection at the Tate Gallery. The circles were sited in a wooded part
of Mrs Kieler's garden at Kingston-on-Thames. Her collection has since
been dispersed, and at Hat Hill we have placed the circles in a clearing
in the trees, as instructed by the artist.

Lynn Chadwick
Stranger III 1959 (cast 1996)
bronze, W 264 cm
Enabled by the Hat Hill Sculpture Foundation

One of only a handful of public commissions undertaken by Chadwick, *Stranger III*, originally commissioned by the Air League of the British Empire, gave him an opportunity to work on a monumental scale. This sculpture was to commemorate the double crossing of the Atlantic by the Airship R 34 in July 1919, and was to be placed outside the Long Haul Terminal at Heathrow Airport.

The architect of the terminal, Frederick Gibberd, the Royal Fine Art Commission, the Minister of Transport, Harold Watkinson, and the Committee of the Air League were all enthusiastic about the sculpture. However, in 1958 an opposing committee led by Lord Brabazon of Tara, who called the sculpture a 'diseased Haddock', with the Guild of Air Pilots and Aviators behind him, forced the Air League to withdraw the commission. Lynn Chadwick made one cast in 1959 which has since been destroyed. Of the declared edition of four, one is sited publicly in Spoleto, Italy, another is at Colby College, Bixler Art and Music Center in Maine and a third in Belgium. Sculpture at Goodwood has completed the edition with this cast made at Chadwick's own foundry, Pangolin Editions, in Gloucestershire from a moulding taken from the piece in Belgium.

The winged figure is a development from the maquette, *Stranger II* 1958. The maquette shows two figures merging with the heads looking both to the left and right, symbolising the double transatlantic journey, with spread symmetrical wings. In the final figure Chadwick has fore-shortened one wing and tapered the other, whilst maintaining a compositional balance.

Bryan Kneale
Deemster Fish 1996
corten steel, L 366 cm
Enabled by the Hat Hill Sculpture Foundation

Deemsters are the judges of the Isle of Man, who, when reciting how they will carry out the laws of the island, promise to do so 'as evenly as the spine of the herring lies between its flesh'. The herring, historically the staple food of the island's people, has become a symbol of good, and Bryan Kneale, himself a Manx man, has used the form of the herring in this sculpture. He was commissioned by the Deemsters to make a sculpture for their court building in Douglas, and he has spent the last eighteen months or so investigating the nature of the fish, and relating it to one of three possible sites in and around the building - a wall, a ceiling and an open outdoor area. He found over fifty possibilities in drawings and in metal models, and decided that a structure to hang on a particular wall in the courthouse was the best solution. The wealth of ideas related to the subject meant that Sculpture at Goodwood was able to help him realise a free-standing version.

Kneale developed the form as an 'inside/outside' structure in which both the exterior and inner workings of the fish were conveyed without being too literal. The many models and drawings he made varied in emphasis from mechanistic, possibly very abstract solutions to others which conveyed more movement. The Goodwood piece is the most abstract. An inclination towards investigating skeleton forms in animals, birds and reptiles is well established in Kneale's vocabulary, and these pieces are both complex and mature.

The model for *Deemster Fish* is exactly like the finished sculpture. Bryan Kneale has a strong sense of scale in his work, which allows his models to be enlarged precisely. The flexibility and resilience found in corten steel allows the form in this sculpture to remain precise - a softer, polished metal would not hold the shapes so exactly.

William Turnbull
Gate 1972
stainless steel, W 292 cm
Private Collection

The gate form is of great interest to William Turnbull, and he had made two other gates in the early 1960s in stone, bronze and wood. When he made this piece some ten years later, he was thinking about the way that the gate squeezes space. The passage through the gate also held great significance. In Japan and India, for example, you pass through temple gates from the outer bustle of everyday life into another type of space which might be calm, quiet, enclosed or very special. For Turnbull the gate can also be the sculptural equivalent to the window for a painter. 'When you are looking through a window you are seeing a very extensive, infinite space viewed through a very limited compressed space, and it was this particular quality that interested me about doing gates.'

Turnbull chose stainless steel for this particular gate as he was at the time experimenting with the material in other work which was to be shown outside. He enjoyed its reflective qualities, and has emphasised them by his treatment of the surface which he finished with a grinder so that it caught the light in different ways. At this time he was very involved with the effect of light on sculpture and had made a number of works in transparent perspex and some open wood structures which were concerned with how light reflected from or filtered through them. At different times of day or in sunlight or cloud cover, *Gate* can be almost white or uniformly grey.

Gate 1972 forms an entrance to the theatre at Hat Hill Copse, and frames the curving rows of seats and a portion of the stage. It also frames the fields beyond, thus capturing both a specific and an infinite space.

Zadok Ben-David

Conversation Piece 1996
bronze, L 366 cm
Enabled by the Hat Hill Sculpture Foundation

Zadok Ben-David first made a sculpture on this theme in 1991. This version is very close to the original, but with subtle alterations. It is slightly larger, the form is altered to greater dynamism, and the small figures are in changed relationships. This new version has been editioned in bronze, whereas the former was made of a metal armature, aluminium and resin, painted.

In the early 1990s, Zadok Ben-David, who had been making animal sculptures with human attributes, turned his thoughts towards the opposite notion: the idea of the beast within man. But there is, in addition, landscape within the form. The horizontal line drawn along the back to the head of this crouched figure forms a horizon on which cavorting figures describe his inner self. Zadok Ben-David has created something he calls an 'inner-scape'. It is not a self-portrait.

This figure was first made as an outline drawing in metal rods, then fleshed out with wire mesh and covered with a textured coating of resin. The inner figures are drawn and cut in aluminium with a jig saw - 'almost quicker than drawing for me now,' says Ben-David. In this case, the whole was then cast in bronze.

The silhouette form is typical of Zadok Ben-David's sculpture. It came from his use of shadows in earlier work, for example, *The Lizard Hunter Who Has Been Followed by His Own Shadow* and *The Marvellous Adventure of A Yellow Elephant*, both of 1985. The shadows were just one element in a work, but have since become the whole sculpture. In their likeness to shadows, these new sculptures are black and have only a hint of three-dimensional form.

Michael Sandle
A Mighty Blow for Freedom: Fuck the Media 1988
bronze, H 220 cm
The Artist

A Mighty Blow for Freedom: Fuck the Media comes towards the end of a particularly fertile period for Sandle during which he produced memorable images of *St George and the Dragon, The Drummer* and *A Woman for Heidelberg* and just before he began work on *A Siege Bell for Malta*. In *A Mighty Blow for Freedom* a powerful androgynous figure, helmeted and muscular, akin to the strong-armed man who strikes the gong in the Rank Organisation's logo, takes a cudgel to a television screen. The sculpture is full of energetic movement and fervour, the kind of zest that was found in Futurism and Vorticism earlier in the century. The influence of Boccioni in *The Drummer* is shown through internalised movement. By contrast, in *A Mighty Blow for Freedom*, Sandle expresses the full force of external motion.

Sandle's contempt for the media is well known, and is succinctly summed up in this powerful image.

Stephen Cox

Granite Catamarans on a Granite Wave 1994
black and white granite, L 800 cm
Commissioned by the Hat Hill Sculpture Foundation

When Stephen Cox first arrived in India in 1985 and travelled to the coastal village of Mahabalipuram, which is devoted to the production of traditional Indian Temple Carving, he was much taken with the fishing boats that were drawn up on the beach, and which, daily, plied a hazardous course in the strong currents of the Indian Ocean. Cox spent several months working with carvers in Mahabalipuram, preparing his own sculpture for the Sixth Indian Triennale, an International exhibition held in New Delhi, and at which he won a major prize.

Cox set up his own studio near the sea on the road between Mahabalipuram and Madras, and has supported a small team of assistants there ever since. Continuing to be interested in the forms of the fishing boats, he bought several of them which he kept at his studio with the thought that one day he might be able to use them. Ten years later the image of these vessels has appeared in this sculpture. The granite catamarans are an exact replica of the wooden craft, carved planks that are bound together with cord. The solution Cox found to indicate the wave was achieved through drawing with a computer, and resulted in a grid of vertical columns made to varying heights. Granite from the quarries at nearby Kanchipuram was selected in two different colours, black for the boats and white for the wave.

Placed at the edge of Hat Hill Copse, the sculpture refers not only to the plantation with its even rows of trees, but also to the distant Channel coastline, as from some angles the boats appear to sit upon the watery horizon. The sculpture marks a new phase in Cox's development, in which he appears to be evolving an interest in sculpture as installation.

Bill Woodrow
Sitting on History I 1990-95
bronze, L 300 cm
Sculpture at Goodwood

Sitting on History I was purchased by Sculpture at Goodwood in celebration of winning the National Art Collections Fund Prize 1996. This work brings together in one piece the strands of our main endeavours, to provide both major sculpture and excellent seating for the interest and enjoyment of our visitors.

This sculpture was proposed in response to a commission first mooted in 1990, and Bill Woodrow's Tate Gallery exhibition in 1996 gave him the opportunity to realise one of three ideas for sculptures which could function as seats. Woodrow had made three maquettes based on a book form: this version, one with coins as the seat backs, and another featuring two crows on the spine of the book fighting over a gold coin. His idea was to have a sculpture that was only completed conceptually and formally when a person sat on it. *Sitting on History I*, with its ball and chain, refers not as one might expect directly to chained libraries, but to the book as the captor of information from which we cannot escape. All of history is filtered through millions of pages of writing, making the book the major vehicle for years of research and study. Woodrow proposes that although we absorb this knowledge, we appear to have great difficulty in changing our behaviour as a result.

The real books from which the original maquettes were made came from a box of books given to Bill Woodrow by a London bookseller, discarded as no longer saleable. To Woodrow's wry amusement, in this haul were three volumes on the history of the Labour Party, which he chose to use for the maquettes. Woodrow finds books one of the most powerful democratic tools in the world and still possibly the most advanced form of communication - perversely more so than computers which seem now to dominate our lives.

Colin Rose
Night and Day 1992
aluminium, H 800 cm
The Artist

A breaking point, the fleeting moment between night and day or dark and light, is celebrated in this sculpture. First made for the Yorkshire Sculpture Park, *Night and Day* was shown about seven metres from the ground in an oak tree, remote from touch but entirely visible. Colin Rose eschews tactile quality in these works in favour of the visual, and although at Sculpture at Goodwood it is possible to touch the sculpture, the lower level gives the viewer a more intimate association with the piece.

Colin Rose likes machined metal with its purity of line to be seen against organic form. The contrast between pale aluminium and the dark background of trees, and static geometric form against natural shape and changing landscape, contributes to the whole experience of the sculpture.

Peter Randall-Page
Secret Life I 1994
granite, L 157 cm
Private Collection

Rock holds the secret of its own history, which is sometimes revealed to us by the fossils it may harbour, or by the explosion or the sedimentary layers which might have formed it. Peter Randall-Page suggests in his *Secret Life* series, of which these boulders form part, that there is always more within: within us, within a stone, within a body or a shell.

In the first of these sliced and carved Finnish granite rocks Peter Randall-Page has revealed curling lines which describe a tree: this surely acknowledges linear foliage motifs found in Celtic design. In the fourth, a nest of smaller rocks appears to have been placed, geometrically, within what has become through his intervention a protective shell - much as crystals grow inside the earth.

There is a marked contrast between the outer, natural boulder, worked through the ages by glacial erosion, and the inner patterns carved in newly exposed stone. The rough and tumble of climate and time have done their work on the outside. The artist has made us aware of these processes, whilst extending our thoughts to the myriad preoccupations, questions and experiences that he has brought to the sculpture at the point of carving the inside. The decorative knots and coils of *Ways to Wrap a Stone I and II*, and *Beneath the Skin*, carved in Kilkenny limestone in 1990 and 1991, showed outer form describing inner possibilities. In the *Secret Life* series, this proposition is reversed.

Eilís O'Connell
Space Emptied Out 1994
stainless steel, corten steel, bronze, H 600 cm
Enabled by the Hat Hill Sculpture Foundation

Space Emptied Out is a conundrum, a brain-teaser, a riddle even.
Here are three objects, containers, whose presence suggest that they
could hold things, perhaps liquids, in the bronze and corten steel
structures. The basket weave of the stainless steel cord figure could
contain solid things. The fact is, they contain nothing, not even
'space', we are told. As we think further, however, the forms themselves
displace space by their mere existence. They occupy a specific area
and the spaces between them are particular and consequently
important to the composition as a whole.

The large and varied grain silos of an agricultural landscape can also
be seen at work in *Space Emptied Out*, found, as here, in intimate
clusters.

Of all the sculpture in the copse this alone defies precise description
or analysis. It is indeed a conundrum.

George Cutts
Sea Change 1996
stainless steel, D 1000 cm
Enabled by the Hat Hill Sculpture Foundation

Imagine that you are swimming in the sea, with the motion of waves causing kelp to sway to and fro. This vision inspired George Cutts to create a series of moving sculptures which captured this kind of motion. *Sea Change* is one of them.

Driven by an electric motor, the curved poles create an undulating movement, causing a change in the space between them as they revolve. The generous, expansive sway in *Sea Change* reflects its organic origin, interesting to contemplate as it is translated through the inorganic medium of stainless steel. The steel poles catch the light as they revolve, again capturing some of the feeling of an underwater world.

George Cutts is an enthusiastic scuba-diver, and has used his observations of sea weed, currents, wave motion and light in many of his sculptures. *The Kiss* 1991, which was exhibited at Sculpture at Goodwood during the first season, was extremely popular with visitors, and whilst it was powered in the same way as *Sea Change*, the more upright poles gave a very different movement - more curving, less swaying than in this sculpture. The motion in both works has a mesmerising quality, much as the tune of the snake charmer's flute mesmerises the cobra.

Stephen Cox

Organs of Action - speech, evacuation,
procreation, grasp, gait 1987-88
black granite, H 187 cm
The Artist

One of the earliest sculptures that Stephen Cox made in India was
Etruscan 1985, four oval heads emerging from slabs of granite to
represent the four senses: taste, sight, hearing and smell. The oval, a
form which has recurred in Cox's sculpture over many years, represents
the 'Cosmic Egg' that floated in the primal waters, according to Hindu
belief, and is used here as a basic sculptural device to support the
features - mouth, eyes, ears and nose.

The extended, vertical oval form is also used in Hindu imagery as a
lingum. Anointed with oil and worshipped, this symbol of male fertility
has been engaged by Cox as a vehicle for the organs of action -
mouth, anus, penis, hands and legs. They stand, taller than man, in
a circle, reminiscent of ancient standing stones, and anointed with oil
as in a *puja* or prayer. The hollow in which the stones are placed at
Hat Hill contains the sculpture perfectly. It was once a flint mine, the
flint stones from which were used in the construction of the fine wall
which encloses two sides of the copse.

Granite is one of the oldest stones in the earth's crust and, for Cox,
bears a mystical significance. It is hard to work, and the artist's
intervention becomes a mark for all time.

William Turnbull
Large Spade Venus 1986
bronze (York stone base), H 187.4 cm
Private Collection

Large Spade Venus, cast 1 of an edition of 4, is typical of Turnbull's work in which he combines the form of a utilitarian object with an elusive kind of figuration.

This sculpture reveals Turnbull's interest in sculpture as metamorphosis. The form comes from somewhere between one thing and another, and we are forced to view it in the way we might look at objects from the past, which, through the passage of time, have taken on the identity of a work of art. Turnbull says, 'We now no longer look at them in relationship to their utility, but for their sculptural quality, perhaps because they were sympathetically formed in the first place.'

Another of the formal aspects of *Large Spade Venus* is the way in which Turnbull has taken a broad form, which from one view is almost confrontational and then in profile is very narrow, almost disappearing. It is his way of twisting space, trying to make it elastic, and is a convention that can be seen in much of his work.

All the sculptures in this edition have the same green patina. Colour is important in Turnbull's work. He feels that certain materials, bronze in particular, take colour well, and the colour chosen has much to do with the emotional content of the work. 'One of the things about bronze is the way that it takes a range of colours that other metals don't.' Red, he felt, would not have been the right colour for this form.

Michael Kenny
In Secrecy and Solitude 1991-92
Portland and Hornton stone (Purbeck stone base), L 200 cm
The Artist

Set with care in a quiet corner of the copse, the circular Purbeck
stone base for *In Secrecy and Solitude* takes the place of the gallery
floor. Indoors Kenny would have drawn concentric circles on the floor
in which to position three geometric forms at random. Here they are
placed in considered relationship with the lines incised in the stone
base. The sculpture is calm, balanced and harmonious, the physical
form giving truth to the spiritual.

Kenny has been working with Portland stone since the early 1980s.
He particularly enjoys the contrast between white limestones, and the
colourful greens and soft golden browns of Hornton stone which comes
from the Midlands, near Banbury, and others which give variety in
texture, colour and finish.

Geometry is put to use in many ways in Michael Kenny's sculpture: to
define shape in line and volume, to achieve balance and proportion
and through this a spirituality, as architects in classical Greece and
artists of the Renaissance have done. Line brings together the diverse
elements in his sculpture, and the geometry gives tranquillity and
calmness.

The notion of movement in such quiet and still work can be found in
Kenny's use of the diagonal, a line rising between the horizontal and
vertical which might also be the line which holds the composition of
the whole in balance.

Nigel Hall
Soglio (Goodwood) 1994
corten steel, L 1100 cm
Enabled by the Hat Hill Sculpture Foundation

Soglio (Goodwood) 1994 was made some time after Nigel Hall had
visited the Alps, and the site that he has chosen for the sculpture at Hat
Hill reflects similar qualities in that landscape: a gap opening up, a far
view, penetrating and broken forms. The rich patina of oxidised steel
and the geometrically formal shapes contrast dramatically with the
changing landscape. The great subtlety of line and angle to be found
in this piece, Hall's largest sculpture to date, ensures that it rests well
in its space. *Soglio* in Italian means throne.

'My work has always been about place, and for Goodwood the
sculpture will echo the fracture in the broken wall,' said Hall, when
planning this work. 'I like the idea of turning back and looking up the
slope of the hill - a sense of engulfing and containment. I am fascinated
by the way geometry can be discerned in landscape, and my preferred
landscapes are mountains or the desert.

'The vertical form is the only vertical in the rolling landscape. It anchors
the sculpture and relates to the viewer's vertical stance. It indicates the
earth's centre. The break in the three wedge forms echoes the angled
break in the long flint wall, while the truncated cone acts both as a lens
and frame to focus and isolate various pockets of landscape.

'It's a meditative space, creating a ground in which the figure of the
vertical can exist in stillness. The sculpture is still when the viewer is still
but active when the viewer moves. For example, when moving across
the face of the sculpture the vertical "knife blade" seems to open and
close suddenly.'

Richard Deacon
When the Landmasses First Appeared 1986
laminated wood and zinc-coated steel, L 750 cm
British Oxygen Corporation

British Oxygen and the Hat Hill Sculpture Foundation have collaborated in the restoration of this sculpture, and before it is returned to the BOC Headquarters at Windlesham in Surrey, it will be exhibited at Sculpture at Goodwood for two years.

When the Landmasses First Appeared has two distinct elements: the zinc-coated steel frame, and the laminated wooden ribbon which snakes around and through it. The fluid, wandering line of the wood contrasts with the rigid metal enclosure, both in form and in material character. Deacon has made the wood rich in texture, with glue like honey oozing between the laminates, whilst the cool, hard steel is static and remorseless. The freely drawn ribbon is to some extent contained by the metal enclosure, even though the rhythms inherent in the wooden structure suggest a desire to escape.

A sculpture about containment, about movement, this relates in form to other contemporary pieces by Deacon, such as *Blind, Deaf and Dumb* 1985 and *Listening to Reason* 1986. In *When the Landmasses First Appeared*, however, the relationships between the forms, and their relationship to the ground, are much more complex. The lightness and freedom of the wood emerges from and writhes around the mineral element, metal formed originally within the earth's crust. In *Richard Deacon* (Phaidon 1995) the artist is quoted as saying, in conversation with Pier Luigi Tazzi, 'When I began making sculptures the procedures that I used were intended to make the act of work create the form and input structure into the material. Structure and material and form were all equally present on the surface: there was no hierarchy between those elements.' There appears to be no hierarchy within this sculpture.

John Maine
Enclosure 1995
Portland stone, D 244 cm
The Artist

Enclosure is a section of a circular column, three-quarters of the circle being enclosed and one quarter open. Made as part of a series of columns, this was the largest of a group of ten exhibited at Winchester Cathedral in 1992. However, typically of John Maine's working practice, when the sculpture had been standing in his studio for several years after the exhibition, he began to work on it again and developed the piece to its current state - to a point where he considers it to be complete.

During the first half of this decade John Maine was also working on other large sculptures devoted to the column form, most significantly the *Doddington Stacks*, of local sandstone, *Strata*, a 30 metre high granite monument in Japan, and *Chiswell Earthworks*, an enormous landscape sculpture of earth and stone built into the Dorset coast. Some of the qualities in these works are to be found in *Enclosure*, most obviously in the column form, but also in the layers which make the structure, and in the treatment of the outer surface. Here the carved, gently undulating pattern unites the separate elements - not precisely, however, as John Maine likes the viewer's eye to make the final leap and therefore the connection. The point at which *Enclosure* becomes different is in the break of the circular form, the place where the artist reveals the interior space. The inside of the sculpture is rough and weathered, much as the stone would appear when cut from the quarry and left in the open air for a long time. The patina of age, with old quarry marks and cuts made by the artist some time ago, contrasts strongly with the freshly carved and textured exterior, where the diagonal ripples add dynamic movement and take the eye around the form. The outside, it would seem, has become the interior.

Ana Maria Pacheco
Requiem 1986-95
Portland stone, slate, bronze, steel, painted, L 750 cm
Enabled by the Hat Hill Sculpture Foundation

It is quite natural to surmise what might be contained in a sealed parcel or a bag. The use of such a device in Ana Maria Pacheco's *Requiem*, however, serves to make us look elsewhere in the sculpture for clues. The pile of slates on which the parcel is placed might suggest some, and the figure, taking a first tentative step away from the ties which attached him to the earth, his eyes fixed to a far horizon, gives us more. Here is an enigma. Like much of Ana Maria Pacheco's other work in sculpture, painting, drawing and printmaking, there is a narrative involved. Characters which inhabit her carefully woven tales are frequently depicted making a journey, and the paraphernalia of travel, a mysterious bag or a box of tricks, is sometimes used in order to intrigue and tease.

Ana Maria Pacheco began work on the sculpture in 1986, as a tribute to her father who had recently died. The carving and final form of assembly were completed at Hat Hill in March 1995 during cold, wet weather with the artist crouching in considerable discomfort under a temporary awning in driving rain. The rain persisted and eventually dissolved the painted stripes on the figure's trunks. Ana Maria Pacheco came back to Hat Hill to repaint them in the early summer; the sun was shining and the work was completed. Apparently this was the only time that she had worked on *Requiem* in good weather.

Sir Anthony Caro
Goodwood Steps 1996
steel, L 31 m 95 cm
Enabled by Sculpture at Goodwood with
acknowledgement to the Henry Moore Sculpture Trust

'*Goodwood Steps* started from a work that I made indoors in Halifax, Yorkshire, and whilst working on this piece I realised that it would be quite different from the Halifax work, which was a sculpture inside a room with a stone floor. Although it was an open form, it was very enclosed within the room. *Goodwood Steps* is a sculpture against a landscape. You can get away from it, see it whole, look at it from above, and you are conscious of the view of the countryside through it and the big sky. However, the sculpture still relates intimately to the viewer. Walking along its length and under the steps one gets a kind of physical experience - something like the way the viewer experienced *The Tower of Discovery* which stood at Sculpture at Goodwood for three years.

'I have been fascinated by the project because it's so architectural. Because of this the piece seems to bear a different relation to us and to the environment from what we normally expect of sculpture. The repetiotion and mechanical elements are a counterpoint to the grand view of the downs - not as in the work of Moore, which was often a reminder of the landscape, but as a contrast to it, much in the way that the mechanical shape of a windmill brings a human dimension to the land.'

This statement was made by Anthony Caro at Hat Hill Copse whilst he was working on the sculpture.

Designers at Sculpture at Goodwood

From the time they established the Hat Hill Sculpture Foundation, Wilfred and Jeannette Cass supported young designers, most of whom are under the age of twenty-five, by purchasing their work. Sculpture at Goodwood continues this practice through commissioning one or two items a year. *The Desk, Seat and Postcard Vending Furniture* by Ben Brooks in the Gallery were made to celebrate the opening of Sculpture at Goodwood in 1994. The swirling rhythms in these pieces stem from Brooks's interest in waves and other water movements which are taken up in the way he manipulates wood and uses its grain.

Tom Heatherwick's *Pavilion*, made whilst he was an undergraduate at Manchester College of Art, his *Five Metre Bench* in laminated plywood and two terrazzo benches, made as a postgraduate at the Royal College of Art, demonstrate his breadth of vision and imaginative use of materials. Through his inspirational vision, utilitarian items become sculpture. Other seats, James Pajet's *Garden Throne*, David Harvey's *Serpentine Seat* and John Greed's *Vertebrae Bench* and *Seat*, are well designed in a variety of materials, and can be purchased directly from their workshops. Johnny Woodford and Alison Crowther work to commission. Both artists also make items in their studios and sell them through exhibitions. Woodford's solidly sculptural *Serpent Bench* and Crowther's *Kissing Seat* with its delicately carved leaf surfaces are typical examples. Alison Crowther has produced a booklet of her designs which guides clients through the range of work that she undertakes. The *Log Cabin*, by students of John Makepeace's Hook College at Parnham in Dorset, was designed as a project for low cost Third World housing. This prototype at Sculpture at Goodwood is made in green wood from Hat Hill Copse. The project has yet to be pursued commercially.

Finally, Steven Gregory's *Sculptural Arrows* blend gently with natural forms in the landscape as they guide visitors through the grounds.

Ben Brooks
Desk 1994
American maple, ash, glass

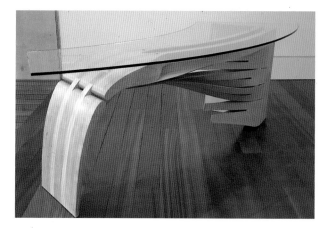

Alison Crowther
Kissing Seat 1995
oak

Craig Downie Architects
Gallery/Reception 1994

John Greed
Vertebrae Bench 1993
South American Hardwood, carbon fibre

Stephen Gregory
Sculptural Arrow 1994
steel, painted

David Harvey
Serpentine Seat 1993
oak and concrete

Thomas Heatherwick
Pavilion 1993
acrylic, wood, aluminium

Thomas Heatherwick
Five Metre Bench 1994
laminated plywood

Thomas Heatherwick
*Bench*1994
terrazo

Students of Hook College

Log Cabin 1993
green wood, plastic

James Pajet
Garden Throne, 1994
aluminium

Johnny Woodford
Serpent Bench, 1993
elm

Sculptors Biographies

Edward Allington

Edward Allington was born in Troutbeck Bridge, Westmorland (now Cumbria) in 1951. He studied at Lancaster College of Art (1968-71), the Central School of Art and Design, London (1971-74) and the Royal College of Art, where he read cultural history (1983-84). He was prizewinner of the John Moore's Liverpool Exhibition (1989) and Gregory Fellow in Sculpture at Leeds University (1989).

Allington's first solo exhibition was at 1b Kensington Church Walk, London, in 1977. Since then his work has been shown frequently, in both mixed and one-man exhibitions in many countries, including Japan, America and throughout Europe. He lives and works in London.

A long-standing interest in Greek and Roman cultures is evident in Edward Allington's sculpture and drawing. References to architectural detail, collectors' artifacts, placement and social context also play their part, and the viewer soon realises that there is a sense of deep enquiry as well as a little mischief at play. In his early work Allington explored a wide variety of materials, but recently he has used copper and bronze, sometimes with other elements, such as photographs of the work in a non-museum context.

Zadok Ben-David

Zadok Ben-David was born in Bayhan, Yemen, in 1949, and was brought up in Israel. He studied at Bezalel Academy of Art and Design, Jerusalem (1971-73), Reading University (1975) and St Martin's School of Art, London (1976). When he moved to London to study he not only had to come to terms with a new verbal language, but also a new visual language - British abstraction and conceptual art of the 1970s was very different from that in Jerusalem. At that time, leading British sculptors such as Anthony Caro, Phillip King and Tim Scott were teaching at St Martin's. After two intensive years of study, Ben-David found himself alone in a Greenwich studio and felt the need to come to terms with his own identity through his work - a search for meaning rather than working intuitively. He acknowledged everything that he found in his adopted culture, but selected carefully those aspects that would bring greater meaning to his work as an artist.

Colour and animal forms are characteristic of Zadok Ben-David's early work. The remembered warmth of the Yemeni desert came through in warm yellows and reds, and the animals, recalled largely through childhood stories, play out their mythical tales. Textured surfaces absorb the light and allow the colours to resonate, and the contrast of matt black shadows allows the forms to flatten. In recent work the role of the animal has altered. Instead of examining anthropomorphic animal activity, Ben-David has turned to looking at the animal in man. Man's beastly qualities are indicated by his stance and actions. Metaphysics has drawn Ben-David to an interest in the alchemist and man's scientific discoveries in the eighteenth and nineteenth centuries. Scientific book illustrations from this time also hold a great interest for him, and have found their way into his installation work. All of these focus on an underlying interest in man, his humanity and his progression in the world.

Sir Anthony Caro

Sir Anthony Caro was born in New Malden, Surrey, in 1924. He studied engineering at Christ's College, Cambridge (1942-44). After National Service with the Fleet Air Arm of the Royal Navy (1944-46), he attended Regent Street Polytechnic Institute, London (1946) and the Royal Academy Schools, London (1947-52).

Caro began to make sculpture after leaving Charterhouse School in Surrey, but parental pressure forced him to take a degree in a subject that would offer a stable career. Subsequently he was supported by his family in his wish to study sculpture. He worked as a part time assistant to Henry Moore (1951-53), and taught part time at St Martin's School of Art, London (1952-1980). There he virtually formed what was to become an influential Department of Sculpture where young artists, following his lead, were working in new materials such as plastic and fibreglass as much as, or more than steel. Students at St Martin's included David Annersley, Phillip King, Tim Scott, William Tucker and many others who were to make significant contributions to the development of sculpture in Britain.

Caro's early sculpture was figurative and expressionistic, worked in clay and cast metals. In 1959, however, he broke away from figuration completely and made works from scrap steel girders and sheet metal, welded and bolted together. Many were coated with industrial and household paints.

His first table sculptures were made in 1966. Smaller than previous work, these were the result of a conversation that Caro had with Michael Fried. The pedestal that he originally rejected was reclaimed in a different form. He continued to make table sculptures well into the 1980s. Meanwhile he was developing his work in steel on a massive scale, some of which is essentially architectural.

In 1993 Caro returned to working with clay in combination with metal and wood (having worked twice before with clay and ceramics) in a series of sculptures describing the Trojan Wars. His first semi-figurative work since the 1950s, its immediate origins lay in a visit to the studio of Hans Spinner in the south of France, where Caro made ceramic forms that were to become the heads of warriors and gods. The resulting installation is a collection of over forty pieces.

Anthony Caro has had numerous significant exhibitions throughout the world, from the first Biennale des Jeunes Artistes in Paris in 1959 where he won the sculpture prize, to his magnificent retrospective exhibition at the Trajan Markets in Rome in 1993. His work is well known and respected from the United States to Japan, and in 1995 a large retrospective exhibition was shown at the new Metropolitan Museum of Art in Tokyo, the museum's first exhibition offered to a foreign artist.

Awarded a knighthood in the Queen's Birthday Honours of 1987, Caro has also received honorary degrees from universities and art schools in Britain and abroad.

Lynn Chadwick

Lynn Chadwick was born in London in 1914. He attended the Merchant Taylor's School, and after taking his School Certificate stayed on to study drawing, watercolour and oil painting. He was then sent to Vouvray to study French. From 1933 to 1939 he trained and worked as an architectural draughtsman in London.

In 1940-41 he worked as a farm labourer and then volunteered for the Fleet Air Arm, becoming a pilot and gaining a commission. After the war he returned to his work with the architect Rodney Thomas, specialising in exhibition design. His early sculptural works took the form of mobiles, which he began to make in 1947, having moved from London to Gloucestershire. A mobile constructed from aluminium and balsa wood was shown at the Aluminium Development Stand at the Builders' Trades Exhibition that year. At this time, and until 1954, he produced textile, furniture and architectural designs.

Chadwick's first one-man exhibition was held at the Gimpel Fils Gallery, London, in 1950, the first of many exhibitions world-wide. These have included the XXVIII Venice Biennale of 1956 where he won the International Sculpture Prize, one of many awards and accolades, including the CBE in 1964. Early in his career he worked occasionally to commission, but less as he became established.

His approach to making sculpture is based in construction rather than modelling. Chadwick first makes a linear armature or skeleton before building on a solid skin. The work might be unique or made to a predetermined edition by casting or fabrication. Chadwick has created a permanent exhibition of his work at his Gloucestershire home, Lypiatt Park, and also a foundry, Pangolin, which casts not only his sculpture but also work for many other artists.

Stephen Cox

Stephen Cox was born in Bristol in 1946. He studied at the Central School of Art and Design, London (1966-68).

Cox's work is based in other cultures. Rooted in classicism, his early sculptures related to architecture and archaic fragments, and were realised in stone from Italian quarries. The Mediterranean as the cradle of civilisation of the Western world provided the context and the substance for his work.

In 1986 Cox represented Britain at the Sixth Indian Triennale in New Delhi. He went to Mahabalipuram, a centre for traditional Hindu carving, to make sculpture for the exhibition, and since that time has maintained a studio there. The carvings he made in granite from the ancient quarries of nearby Kanchipuram were to have a great bearing on his work over the next decade. Some were more overtly 'Indian' than others, and might be viewed as being linked to the humanism of both the Eastern and Western worlds.

Another opportunity for Cox to work in a new context, this time in Egypt, presented itself in 1988. He was commissioned to carve sculpture for the new Cairo Opera House, and was allowed to quarry Imperial porphyry at Mons Porphyrytes in the Eastern Desert, which had not been used since the Renaissance. This in turn led to new developments in his imagery, such as references to the human torso. In varying his treatment of the rich red and green stones, Cox developed his sculpture towards a more abstract state. In 1993 he completed a commission for the parish church of St Paul, Harringay, using Italian and Egyptian stones.

Cox continues to work in Egypt and has been given permission to quarry stone from another ancient site, the Kephren Quarries in the Western Desert of southern Egypt.

116

Tony Cragg

Tony Cragg was born in Liverpool in 1939. He worked as a laboratory technician at the Natural Rubber Producers Research Association (1966-68) before attending Gloucestershire College of Art and Design, Cheltenham, and the Royal College of Art, London (1973-77). Tony Cragg has lived and worked in Wuppertal, Germany, since 1977.

An artist of great international acclaim and immense energy, Cragg has developed more possibilities in the making of sculpture than any other sculptor since Moore discovered the 'hole' as positive space. He has employed more materials than most, and tested them to their limits through a wide variety of means, so that he seems to be one hundred sculptors at any one time. However, the continuum in his work is strong and uncompromising. His concerns are for humanity, its direction, the life of our planet and its projected evolution. Cragg's contribution to the debate on contemporary sculpture practice is considerable, and has yet to be measured.

Early works of the 1970s were mostly made with found objects through which Cragg questioned and tested possibilities. Later pieces, sometimes derived from found materials, demonstrated a shift of interest to surface quality and how that could be manipulated, and a play with unlikely juxtapositions of materials. Results vary from the exquisite to the grotesque, from the refined to the crude, in bronze, steel, plastic, rubber, glass, wood, plaster and more.

George Cutts

George Cutts was born in Rugby in 1938. On leaving school he worked at Goole Shipyard, and whilst there qualified to attend art school. He studied at Doncaster School of Art (1956-58) and at the Royal College of Art, London (1958-60), under John Skeaping.

He has taught at the Royal College of Art, the Royal Academy Schools, Chelsea and Ravensbourne Schools of Art, Trent and Portsmouth Polytechnics, but now devotes all of his time to making sculpture. He has exhibited in Europe and America, and has undertaken many public commissions in Britain and abroad.

Of his work, George Cutts writes: 'I work directly in stone and stainless steel, the opposing materials with such diverse textural qualities interplay, emphasising my ideas. I am mainly influenced by landscape, although many forms subconsciously revert back to the shipyard, for example, large propellers, ribs, curved forms. The mobiles are derived from water movement and are carefully timed to calm and tranquillise the viewer.'

Richard Deacon

Richard Deacon was born in Bangor, Wales, in 1949. He studied at Somerset College of Art, Taunton (1968), St Martin's School of Art, London (1970-73) and the Royal College of Art (1974-77) where he gained an MA in Environmental Media.

Working both on a domestic and monumental scale, Richard Deacon combines the essence of human form with elements of engineering in his precisely made structures of wood, metal and occasionally, plastics. Metals are riveted together in sweeping shapes which refer to both inner and outer parts of the anatomy, and wood is laminated, bent and twisted into unlikely ribbons and smoothed to solid perfection in more volumetric states.

Public commissions in many countries have given Richard Deacon opportunities to work on an immense scale. *Moor* 1990 at Victoria Park in Plymouth sits high next to a bridge, and is 247 metres long. He also makes works for a particular occasion, for example objects which are used in contemporary dance performances. In 1993 he collaborated with Hervé Robbe in *Factory*, designing the sets and, with Dominique Fabrègue, the costumes. The dance was performed at La Ferme du Buisson, Paris, before touring France. Deacon's use of performance in his work has undergone change throughout his career. He actively participated in his earlier works but eventually found his physical presence became unnecessary. His work evolves with his thinking, in that he does not establish a set of rules or problems to be solved through a predetermined pattern - the ideas rove with the making process.

Richard Deacon has exhibited widely throughout the world with solo exhibitions, and in significant international surveys such as *Documenta IX* in 1992. He was awarded the Turner Prize in 1987. He lives and works in London.

Eva Drewett

Eva Drewett was born in Warsaw in 1957. She came to England in 1979 and studied at Chelsea School of Art, London (1982-83), the Central School of Art and Design (1983-87) and the Royal College of Art (1987-89).

Working mostly in bronze, and recently in steel, Eva Drewett uses the human form to convey a powerful message, not a unique notion in itself, but with a vision that is wrought by some of the harsher realities of life. The forms she finds within apparently limited means are confrontational, sometimes terrifying, and with a presence that cannot be ignored. Whilst delving into mankind's collective psyche, she explores the form of the head or torso with astonishing skill and an uncanny insight into human frailty.

Drewett is at the dawn of her career, but has already had solo exhibitions in Britain and has undertaken a commission for the Royal Hong Kong Jockey Club at Kowloon Sculpture Park.

Ian Hamilton Finlay

Ian Hamilton Finlay was born in Nassau, Bahamas, in 1925. As a child he was brought to Scotland, where he attended boarding school. His education ended at the age of thirteen, when at the outbreak of war he was evacuated to the Orkney Islands.

A short spell at art school in Glasgow was followed by a period in London before Finlay joined the army in 1942. At the end of the war, he worked as a shepherd, studied philosophy, and began to write short stories and plays, some of which were broadcast by the BBC.

Much of Finlay's work has been made in collaboration with other artists and with artisans, and draws on his experience of rural life and the sea. His studies of classicism and ancient philosophers have enriched his work immeasurably.

At Stonypath, near Edinburgh, his home since 1966, Finlay has developed the garden to feature his concrete poetry and sculpture. Although he has gained a considerable international reputation through numerous exhibitions abroad, Ian Hamilton Finlay never travels away from his home.

Laura Ford

Laura Ford was born in Cardiff in 1961. She studied at Bath Academy of Art (1978-82) and at Chelsea School of Art (1982-83).

Her first solo exhibition was held at Nicola Jacobs Gallery in London, since when she has had further solo shows at Benjamin Rhodes Gallery, the Castle Museum, Nottingham, the José Friere Project Space, New York, in 1994, and Spacex, Exeter, in 1996. Her work has also been included in group exhibitions since 1982, mostly in Britain but also in Japan.

Laura Ford's sculpture and prints lie within a world inhabited by children who wish to be seen and admired, yet at the same time to hide from view. These naughty nursery inhabitants evolved from drawings of a tyrannical baby, and were followed by *Bang Bang*, two party dressed and balaclavaed terrorist girls with guns (now in the Arts Council Collection). *Twiglet* followed - a twig headed girl in a black frock, also with guns but encircled by seven sniffing shaggy dogs, then *Stump Girl* and the other *Nature Girls* which are described on page 32.

Recent prints include the images of pretty little girls hiding in foliage, and a strident baby, the Fairy Liquid symbol of gentle strength. The resulting images entirely belie their origins. Sentimentality is overridden whilst Laura Ford allows unease and power struggles to creep in.

Dame Elisabeth Frink

Dame Elisabeth Frink was born in Thurlow, Suffolk, in 1930. She studied at Guildford School of Art (1947-49) and Chelsea School of Art, London (1949-53) under Bernard Meadows and Willi Soukop. She taught at Chelsea School of Art (1953-61), St Martin's School of Art (1954-62) and was visiting lecturer at the Royal College of Art (1965-67).

As one of Britain's leading sculptors, Frink was awarded Honorary Doctorates by the University of Surrey (1977), Open University (1983), University of Warwick (1983), University of Cambridge (1988), University of Exeter (1988), University of Oxford (1989) and University of Keele (1989). She also received official recognition, being awarded the CBE in 1969, and in 1982 she was created Dame of the British Empire.

Men, dogs, horses and birds were constant subject-matter throughout Frink's career. She modelled, cast in plaster and then carved the plaster, much as Henry Moore had done, to achieve a tougher surface when the plaster was cast in bronze. Unlike Moore, however, she rarely worked with the female form: 'I have focused on the male because to me he is a subtle combination of sensuality and strength with vulnerability,' Frink is quoted as saying in the catalogue raisonné of her work (*Elisabeth Frink: Sculpture*, Harpvale, 1984).

Her figures have dignity, mystery and a simplicity of form which place them apart from us: they seem to be focused elsewhere. The animals demonstrate her deep understanding of their state, for she encapsulates their innate and individual characteristics. Frink's drawing and graphic work followed the same themes, being executed with the economy of means and feeling for surface texture that is to be found in her three-dimensional work. Elisabeth Frink died in 1993.

Bruce Gernand

Bruce Gernand was born in America in 1949. He studied at
Pennsylvania State University (1966-68), San Francisco State College
(1968-70) where he gained a BA in Philosophy, City and Guilds of
London Art School (1971-72), the Central School of Art and Design
(1972-74) and the Royal College of Art (1975-76). He has received
awards from the Arts Council (1977) and Eastern Arts Association
(1987), and a Henry Moore Foundation Fellowship (1992-94).
Gernand has exhibited his work regularly in Britain since 1982.
His sculpture was included in the Osaka Triennale of Sculpture 1995,
his first international exhibition.

In scale Bruce Gernand's sculpture relates to the human body, whether
as a mask, or a form that you can measure yourself against or encircle
with your arms. Gernand is concerned with surface and inner shape,
with setting up propositions within his work and dismantling them. He
exploits characteristics of the materials and processes he uses, to the
extent that material and process become the subject of his sculptures.
Plaster, clay, wax, hardboard, wood and metals including aluminium
and bronze, have all been the subject of his questioning application.

Bruce Gernand professes not to want his work to be easily read,
but does not deny the viewer options. A piece might simultaneously
be futuristic and primitive, humorous and sinister, technological and
organic, brutish and vulnerable, positive and negative. Having made
our choice, we are encouraged to think as the artist does, in the
opposite direction.

Andy Goldsworthy

Andy Goldsworthy was born in Cheshire in 1956 and was brought up in Yorkshire. He studied at Bradford College of Art (1974-75) and Preston Polytechnic (1975-78).

After leaving college Goldsworthy lived in Yorkshire, Lancashire and Cumbria. He moved over the border to Langholm, Dumfriesshire, in 1985 and to Penpont one year later. This gradual drift northwards was due to a way of life over which he did not have complete control. However, contributing factors were opportunities and desires to work in these areas and reasons of economy.

Throughout his career most of Goldsworthy's work has been made in the open air, in places as diverse as the Yorkshire Dales, the Lake District, Grize Fiord in the Northern Territories of Canada, the North Pole, Japan, the Australian outback, St Louis, Missouri and Dumfriesshire. The materials he uses are those to hand in the remote locations he visits: twigs, leaves, stones, snow and ice, reeds and thorns. Most works are ephemeral but demonstrate, in their short life, Goldsworthy's extraordinary sense of play and of place. The works are recorded as photographs. Book publication is an important aspect of Andy Goldsworthy's work: showing all aspects of the production of a given work, each publication is a work of art in its own right.

Some recent sculpture has a more permanent nature, being made in stone and placed in locations far from its point of origin, as for example *Herd of Arches* 1994. The series of chalk *Arches* made at Sculpture at Goodwood in 1995 are semi-permanent, given the fragility of the material, and are now sited indoors at Goldsworthy's studio in Dumfriesshire, to extend their life.

Steven Gregory

Steven Gregory was born in Johannesburg, South Africa, in 1952. He studied at St Martin's College of Art, London (1970-72), returning there to complete his BA (Hons) (1977-79). During the intervening years he was an apprentice stonemason, working at Westminster Abbey and Hampton Court. He obtained City and Guilds Craft and Advanced Craft Certificates in stone masonry (1975 and 1976). In 1977 he won the Worshipful Company of Masons Prize.

Stone carving features largely in Steven Gregory's sculpture, although he has also developed ideas in bronze and other media. His intention is to make work that cannot be disregarded, which sometimes results in harrowing images of the human condition. There is also a lighter side to his work where his humour emerges, although the viewer should still search in the shadows for there might still lurk the black dimension.

Charles Hadcock

Charles Hadcock was born in Derby in 1965. He studied at Gloucestershire College of Arts and Technology (1984-87) and at the Royal College of Art, London (1987-89). His degree show at the Royal College generated a good deal of interest in his work, and many encouraging comments in the press. The ideas he was then trying out in his sculpture - using multiple images and explorations of the ready-made - remain important in his work today. A background in engineering (his father was an engineer), an abiding interest in Victorian engineering and in mathematics have enriched those original preoccupations, and are all present in his current work. His is not entirely a cool and calculated art, but one that also has analogies with poetry and music.

Transformation also plays its part. Polystyrene packaging might be cast in bronze and repeated as a multiple (it is a multiple in the first place), artificial paving stones - mass produced - are found giving texture and repetitive form in some sculptures. The nuts and bolts of nineteenth-century engineered bridges are celebrated in his work, giving the underside of the sculpture equal importance with the rest. Geometry also plays a part, in particular the Golden Section, based on the coordinates of Hadcock's own body, as do the rhythm, pause, crescendos and calm of music. All of this culminates in bronze or cast iron. Hadcock uses factory casting for his sculpture in preference to fine art foundries, as he likes the basic qualities of the factory processes to come through in the sculpture, and in particular revels in the qualities of cast iron.

Charles Hadcock has exhibited regularly in group shows since 1987, and has had one-man exhibitions at 249 Long Lane, London (1991), the Crypt Galley, London (1992) and Reeds Wharf Gallery, London (1996). His work can be seen at BAA Gatwick Stirling Hotel, Melbourne Science Park, Cambridgeshire, ICI, and Allied Domecq.

Nigel Hall

Nigel Hall was born in Bristol in 1943. He studied at the West of England College of Art, Bristol (1960-64) and the Royal College of Art, London (1964-67). On graduating from the Royal College, Hall won a Harkness Fellowship, and until 1969 he lived and worked in Los Angeles, travelling in the USA, Canada and Mexico. His work is represented in numerous public, corporate and private collections in Britain and abroad. Hall's first one-man exhibition was held at the Galerie Givaudan, Paris, in 1967. It is interesting to note that fifty out of his seventy-two solo exhibitions held between 1967 and 1996 have been in galleries abroad in cities spread throughout the globe: New York, Los Angeles, Perth, Melbourne, Sydney, Tokyo, Zurich, Dusseldorf, Cologne and Rome, to mention only a few. This inter-national exposure has led to his work being represented in around 100 public and corporate collections and numerous private collections abroad and in Britain.

In 1970 Nigel Hall produced his first tubular aluminium sculptures in which he explored ways of encapsulating space in a linear manner, thus manipulating our perceptions of it. A sense of place and placement have always been integral to his work, and shadows play a role equal to that of line, mass or void, as do changes of aspect from altered viewpoints. An almost minimal refinement and economy of means in Hall's work has recently given way to robust forms which still remain very carefully considered in their configuration. These refer obliquely to mountain landscape which alters dramatically when the viewer moves within it. Site specific projects have also featured regularly during Nigel Hall's career. These include a wall sculpture for the entrance to the Australian National Gallery, Canberra, 1992; a two-part wall relief in painted and gilded wood for the entrance of Providence Towers, Dallas, 1989; and a free-standing steel sculpture for the entrance to Thameslink Road Tunnel, London Docklands, 1993, his largest structure to date.

Shirazeh Houshiary

Shirazeh Houshiary was born in Shiraz, Iran, in 1955. She studied at Chelsea School of Art, London (1976-79) and then for a year was junior fellow at Cardiff College of Art. Her first solo exhibition was held at the Chapter Arts Centre, Cardiff, in 1980, since when she has exhibited regularly in solo and mixed exhibitions in Britain, Europe and America. Houshiary was nominated for the Turner Prize in 1994.

Her sculpture is rooted in the mysticism of Islamic culture, but demonstrates a quest beyond cultural limitations. Treading as she does the path between poetry and the material world, Houshiary achieves an energy in her work which assumes inner light and outer strength.

Michael Kenny

Michael Kenny was born in Liverpool in 1941. He studied at Liverpool College of Art (1959-61) and the Slade School of Fine Art, London (1961-64). Throughout the 1970s he was a visiting lecturer at the Slade School and from 1983 to 1988 was Head of the Fine Art Department at Goldsmith's College, London. Since he graduated from the Slade, Kenny has had many solo and group exhibitions in Britain and abroad, including Europe, USA, South America, Japan, Hong Kong and Australia. Consequently, many public and corporate collections throughout the world hold examples of his work.

The creative acts of drawing and making sculpture seem, in Michael Kenny's work, to be indivisible. The physical qualities of line are to be celebrated, whether drawn on smooth or textured paper or across a piece of stone, whether made in graphite or coloured pigment. 'Drawing', for Kenny, 'is a means of understanding, of searching for order out of chaos through images.' Geometry, symmetry and asymmetry are concerns, both in drawing and in sculpture. Stones with differing qualities are sometimes brought together in one piece, the grainy dark greens and browns of Hornton stone contrasting with the cool, smooth texture of Portland stone or the warmer hue of Bath limestone. Recently Kenny has introduced blue-grey Killkenny marble and white Carrara marbles into his compositions, adding to the range of colour and surface quality in his sculpture. Strong diagonals and verticals in both solid form and in line, pull our attention towards the notions of gravity which are also vital in his work.

Michael Kenny was elected Associate of the Royal Academy in 1976 and Royal Academician in 1986. He lives and works in London.

Phillip King

Phillip King was born in Tunis in 1934. He studied modern languages at Christ's College, Cambridge (1954-57) and sculpture at St Martin's School of Art, London (1957-58) where Anthony Caro was teaching at the time, after which he spent a year working as assistant to Henry Moore.

King has been making sculpture since 1953. Early work was small, made in clay and plaster, and has been described as being of a robust, Brutalist and Surrealist nature. In 1962 he started to use fibreglass and colour (with *Rosebud*), which gave way to both large and small scale metal sculpture, often coloured, and in combination with different materials such as plastic, slate and wood. Work made since 1989 shows a return to figurative sculpture and has almost entirely been cast in bronze.

Phillip King has an established international reputation, having worked in Japan and America, and has exhibited widely overseas, notably representing Britain, with Bridget Riley, at the Venice Biennale in 1968. His work is well represented in public and private collections throughout the world.

Awarded the CBE in 1974, Phillip King was elected Associate of the Royal Academy in 1977 and Royal Academician in 1990.

Bryan Kneale

Bryan Kneale was born in Douglas on the Isle of Man in 1930. His early ambition was to be a painter, and he studied at Douglas School of Art (1947) and at the Royal Academy Schools (1948-52). In 1948 he won the Rome Prize, and spent most of his time travelling in Italy where he was greatly influenced by the work of the Futurists and metaphysical painters. On his return to London in 1951 he started painting with palette knives with a desire to construct in paint, the foundation of his gradual move towards working entirely in three dimensions. In 1960, having learnt welding techniques, Kneale abandoned painting and had his first exhibition of sculpture later that year.

Bryan Kneale has mostly constructed, forged and cast his sculpture himself. He has taught sculpture at the Royal Academy Schools, Hornsey College of Art and the Royal College of Art, where he was Senior Fellow in 1995, the year of his retirement.

His work is largely centred on organic form. Skeletons and joints of animals are explored through drawing and construction in metal. Kneale prefers to work directly in metal rather than modelling in an intermediary material before casting in bronze.

Exhibitions include regular one-man shows since 1953 and group exhibitions since 1961. Kneale has shown mostly in Britain, with occasional exhibitions abroad, although his work is represented in collections from Australia and New Zealand to Brazil and New York. In Britain his drawings can be found in the Natural History Museum and the British Museum, and his sculpture at the Tate Gallery and in many municipal and private collections.

Bryan Kneale was elected ARA in 1970 and Royal Academician in 1974. He lives and works in London.

Richard Long

Richard Long was born in Bristol in 1945. He studied at the West of England College of Art, Bristol (1962-66) and at St Martin's School of Art, London (1966-68).

As early as 1994 Long made his first work involving landscape, which had developed by 1967 towards using distance, in the form of long walks, and space - the open air, aspects of the landscape with his subtle intervention. The element of time became important as he made sculptures by walking, hitch-hiking or bicycling on a predetermined route which might be described as a line or circle on a map. The records of these walks exist as maps, photographs and short, descriptive texts. He has travelled the world making his work, in the Americas, Europe, Africa, Nepal, Australia and Japan a solitary occupation, on occasions involving great hardship and discomfort.

Long's work is highly regarded and he has held many significant one-man exhibitions throughout the world. In 1976 he represented Britain at the Venice Biennale with an installation in the British Pavilion made of marble selected from an Italian quarry.

His practice of making installations in poetic harmony with the buildings in which they are placed has led Long to work in such diverse venues as the Henry Moore Studios at Dean Clough, Halifax, with pieces of coal arranged in a dense black circle, and in 1994, the Sao Paulo Bienal, Brazil, where he used mud from the Amazon splashed in controlled sweeps on the gallery surfaces. In 1989 he was the winner of the Turner Prize.

Richard Long lives in Bristol and continues to travel the world to make his work.

David Mach

David Mach was born in Methil, Fife, in 1956. He studied at Duncan Jordanstone College of Art (1974-79) and at the Royal College of Art, London (1979-82). A random look at his biography shows a life full of activity. For example, in 1989 there are listed twelve exhibitions or installations in ten different cities, ranging from San Francisco to Madrid and Milton Keynes to Melbourne. This is typical of his hectic work pattern which built up to this pitch within four years of his leaving the Royal College, and continues unabated.

Multiple mass-produced objects, most notably magazines, newspapers and car tyres, have been used consistently by Mach throughout his career. He brings diverse items together in large-scale installations with humour and social comment. His work is representational and controversial. A work of the early 1980s, *Polaris* 1983, shown at the Hayward Gallery in London, took the form of a submarine, but made of used car tyres. This monumental tribute to nuclear power was set alight by highly critical viewers who obviously failed to see its irony.

David Mach's sculpture is on the verge of being completely overwhelming in its scale and audacity. Classical pillars made from thousands of newspapers and magazines at the Tramway Gallery in Glasgow in 1990 was a marathon of physical effort in which he was helped, as in much of his work, by his wife Lesley. Papers were fanned and stacked around existing supporting pillars in the tram sheds, transforming them to the scale and form of columns that would support the Acropolis. He also uses magazines to form swirling waves which carry other objects in their turbulence. The density of these installations is echoed in his smaller sculptures where multiple objects are used to make the whole. Typical are the 'match head' series: portraits, similar to Chinese and Venetian theatre masks, made from unstruck matches glued together so that only the coloured heads show on the surface. Sometimes these are fired to form faces of a sombre hue.

John Maine

John Maine was born in Bristol in 1942. He studied at the West of England College of Art, Bristol (1960-64) and at the Royal College of Art, London (1964-67), where he was a contemporary of Nigel Hall, Ken Draper and John Panting. A two-year Fellowship at Gloucestershire College of Art followed. Travels in the Yukutan, Mexico, had an early influence on his work, and he developed the ideas generated there during the course of his fellowship at the Yorkshire Sculpture Park (1979-80), the first artist to be accorded that honour. He then lived in London, with periods of time spent in Dorset working on Portland stone and in Italy working in the famous marble quarries of Carrara.

His first one-man exhibition was held at the Serpentine Gallery in London in 1972, since when he has exhibited regularly in Britain. He has also received many awards, amongst which are the Royal College of Art Drawing Prize (1967), Art Council Awards (1972, 1975 and 1977), the Mark Rothko Memorial Trust award (travel to USA and Mexico, 1979), an Elephant Trust Award for Chiswell Earthworks (1990-95) and a Henry Moore Foundation Award (1991). John Maine was elected Royal Academician in 1995.

Much of John Maine's work has been in the form of public commissions, notably the Chiswell Earthworks in Portland, Dorset (1986-93), the Lewisham 2000 project (from 1991) and his largest sculpture to date, the monument commemorating the completion of the Ryugasaki New Town Hokuryudai Area Development in Japan (1993). Landscape, land forms, ancient sites, structures within nature, mathematical systems, solids, surface planes and sections through forms, all have their place in John Maine's vocabulary as a sculptor. Stone, and in particular Portland stone from Dorset where he lives, is his preferred medium.

Bernard Meadows

Bernard Meadows was born in Norwich in 1915. He studied painting at Norwich School of Art (1934-37). Between 1936 and 1939, and again between 1946 and 1948, he was studio assistant to Henry Moore. He moved to London in 1937, and attended lectures at the London Institute of Education and the Courtauld Institute of Art, and painting and sculpture courses at the Royal College of Art (1938-48).

He served with the RAF (1941-46), initially in Dover and then in India, Ceylon, and in the Cocos Islands in the Indian Ocean. The world at war provided a background of insecurity, vulnerability and terror. Meadows's sculpture inevitably reflected these feelings, which have remained within his work throughout his career. On a more immediate level his keen observation of crabs in the Cocos Islands also had a lasting effect on the imagery he employs in his sculpture. Frightened birds, crab forms and vulnerable figures (protected by hard shells or armour) are constant themes in his sculpture and drawing.

Meadows taught at Chelsea School of Art, London (1948-60), and was Professor of Sculpture at the Royal College of Art (1960-80). He was appointed Professor Emeritus at the Royal College of Art in 1980. As Acting Director of the Henry Moore Foundation (1983-88) he ensured that Moore's work was enlarged in the spirit that Moore intended, and he helped to develop the generous support for artists that the Foundation continues to give today. Since 1989 he has been consultant to the Foundation. The time that Meadows spent teaching and helping artists may account for his relatively small output.

The XXVI Venice Biennale of 1952 brought his name into international prominence and his 80th Birthday Exhibition at the Yorkshire Sculpture Park in 1995 underlined his contribution to the development of sculpture in Britain.

David Nash

David Nash was born in Esher, Surrey, in 1945. He studied at Kingston College of Art (1963-64), Brighton College of Art (1964-67) and Chelsea School of Art (1969-70).

In 1970 he moved to Blaenau Ffestiniog where he lives and works; in that year he made his first wooden tower, since destroyed by a gale.

Nash works entirely in wood - wood that no longer has a useful life - and with living plants. Most of his museum exhibitions have been made in wood which was found in the locality of the host museums, ensuring a relevance which is unique and which neatly sidesteps the notion of being site specific in the traditional sense.

David Nash has worked regularly abroad, particularly in Japan, and enjoys considerable international acclaim, with work represented in numerous collections throughout the world.

Paul Neagu

Paul Neagu was born in Bucharest, Romania, in 1938. He studied at the Institute 'N Grigorescu' (1959-65). In 1969 he came to Britain at the invitation of Richard Demarco, and has since lived and worked in London, as a lecturer in fine art, in addition to pursuing his own career as an artist. Neagu gained British citizenship in 1977.

Paul Neagu's sculpture conveys the notion of movement through abstract form. His drawings, paintings, performances and sculpture are closely linked, in that all explore ideas that cannot be made literal in any concrete sense. They invite participation, which is demanding of the viewer's concentration, and need time as well as space to work their way into our consciousness. Star forms and geometric shapes, often made in stainless steel, with the surface worked to textures that capture and refract light, are typical of Neagu's genre.

Eilís O'Connell

Eilís O'Connell was born in Derry, Northern Ireland, in 1953. She studied at Crawford School of Art, Cork (1970-74), Massachusetts College of Art, Boston (1974-75) and again at Crawford School of Art (1975-77). Two fellowships followed: the Arts Council of Northern Ireland British School at Rome Fellowship (1983-84) and the Arts Council PS1 (New York) Fellowship (1987-88).

A distinctive sense of place that Eilís O'Connell manifests in her work may possibly have led her towards undertaking many important public commissions, mostly in urban settings. These include *Secret Station* 1991, for Cardiff Bay Art Trust at the Eastern Gateway, Cardiff, and *The Space Between* 1992, commissioned by the Milton Keynes Development Corporation. During 1994 and 1995 Eilís O'Connell worked on the design for a lifting footbridge in collaboration with Ove Arup. The bridge will span the River Frome at Narrow Quay in central Bristol.

O'Connell's ability to ensure a successful interaction between the object and its environment may well be rooted in her experience of the Irish landscape in which she grew up. *Secret Station*, however, referred to her experience of the British industrial landscape. Her use of steam in this piece, which was pumped out through fissures in large conical forms, a device she first used in 1990, demonstrates her response to factory chimneys and other industrial outlets.

Eilís O'Connell is particularly concerned with the notions of space within objects, spaces between them and, in turn, their spatial relationship to their place. Materials and processes are also carefully chosen, both for their appropriateness and to convey contrast or emphasis.

Ana Maria Pacheco

Ana Maria Pacheco was born in Goias, Brazil, in 1943. She studied
sculpture at the University of Goias (1963-64) while at the same time
studying music at the Federal University of Goias. This was followed by
further studies in music and other subjects at the University of Brazil,
Rio de Janiero, in 1965.

In 1966 she returned to Goias where she lectured at the School of Fine
Arts and the School of Architecture at the University of Goias, and at
the Institute of Art at the Federal University there until 1973. In 1973
Ana Maria Pacheco left Brazil for Britain. Here, with the support of a
British Council Scholarship, she studied under the figurative sculptor,
Reg Butler, at the Slade School of Fine Art in London until 1975.
Since that time she has developed her career as a sculptor, painter and
printmaker in Britain. Teaching posts have included being Head of Fine
Art at Norwich School of Art, Norfolk, from 1985 to 1989.

From 1980 Ana Maria Pacheco has exhibited world-wide. In Britain
significant exhibitions include the Hayward Annual (1982), and solo
exhibitions in the Icon Gallery, Birmingham (1983), Camden Arts
Centre, London, and the Museum of Modern Art, Oxford (1991), the
Gas Hall, Birmingham Museum and Art Gallery (1994) and the City
of Plymouth Museums and Art Gallery (1995).

Life is a series of journeys, and the most significant so far for Ana
Maria Pacheco must have been her transition from Central Brasil to
Britain. It took a long time for her, having made this drastic change,
to find her way within her work. Journeying is a recurrent theme in
Pacheco's work, together with mysterious narratives, melodramatic
encounters, sexuality, death, power, magic and secrets.

Vong Phaophanit

Vong Phaophanit was born in 1961 in Laos (since 1975 People's Democratic Republic of Laos). He was educated in France (1972-80), and studied painting at the Ecole des Beaux-Arts, Aix-en-Provence (1980-85). Being separated from his family, who remained in Laos from 1973 to 1993, when they were able to visit him in England, possibly led Vong Phaophanit to include photographs of them in some of his earlier work. Not surprisingly, memory plays an important part in his work, as do some of the materials he uses; bamboo, rubber and rice, for example, are significant because of their Asian origin.

Installation, with its origin in Dada and Surrealism, whether using small parts of a space, or a whole room, is his current way of working. His bamboo installation at the Chisenhale Gallery, London, in 1991 brought together light, movement, Laotian text (on the ceremonial gateway through which one entered the installation) and sound as the bamboos rattled together when disturbed. Since then Vong Phaophanit has frequently used Laotian text in his work. The nine red neon words of Litterae Lacentes (Light Writing) at Killerton Park, Devon, in 1993 were placed on a garden wall where bamboo and palm trees had been planted. He did not translate the words for his audience, thus keeping much of the power of the work to himself.

Vong Phaophanit exhibits regularly, both in Britain and abroad. He was shortlisted for the Turner Prize at the Tate Gallery in 1993, where he exhibited his famous *Neon Rice Field*, mounds of rice in straight lines covering white neon lights. The translucency of the rice caused the mounds to glow around the central, brighter neon core. *Azure Neon Body,* his installation at Sculpture at Goodwood, shows a continued interest in language, light and the painterly qualities that can be manifest in materials other than paint. Vong Phaophanit lives and works in Exeter, and is visiting lecturer at Chelsea College of Art, London.

Peter Randall-Page

Peter Randall-Page was born in Essex in 1954. He studied at
Bath Academy of Art (1973-77) before moving to London where
he worked with Barry Flanagan for a year. He was then involved in
the conservation of thirteenth-century sculpture at Wells Cathedral,
Somerset. In 1980 he was awarded the Winston Churchill Memorial
Trust Travelling Fellowship to study marble carving in Italy.

Randall-Page was visiting lecturer in Sculpture at Brighton Polytechnic
from 1982 to 1989, but now devotes his time to his own work at his
studio in Devon.

In 1989 Peter Randall-Page began 'Local Distinctiveness', a project
concerned with placing sculpture in the environment with particular
care for its relevance and sensitive siting. He has exhibited his work
regularly in Britain and abroad.

Natural forms such as shells, fossils, fruits, eggs and pods, as well
as expressive knots and coils, are frequent vehicles for Peter Randall-
Page's ideas. He works mainly in stone, finding carving to be a
sympathetic process that enables him to realise these contemplative
forms.

Colin Rose

Colin Rose was born in Newcastle upon Tyne in 1950. He studied at Newcastle upon Tyne Polytechnic (1973-76) and undertook post-graduate studies in sculpture at Newcastle University (1977-79).

The hallmark of Colin Rose's work is that he uses trees in which to place it. In his early work he found 'homes' for objects in the trees around his studio, but in 1984, with an opportunity to exhibit at the Yorkshire Sculpture Park, he considered the idea of the tree being a place in the landscape, offering a harmony with the elements. This in turn related his work to the landscape. His often large-scale metal or wooden structures either thread their way through the leaves or nestle in the cleft of a branch. With these sculptures Rose seeks to complete the composition of trees that have been thrown into visual imbalance by losing branches or sustaining some kind of damage in the past.

Colin Rose works frequently to commission, and has exhibited regularly in Britain and at times in Europe.

Michael Sandle

Michael Sandle was born in Weymouth, Dorset, in 1936. He studied at Douglas School of Art and Technology, Isle of Man (1951-54), and then did National Service in the Royal Artillery until 1956. During that time he attended evening classes at Chester College of Art. He studied printmaking at the Slade School of Fine Art, London, under Anthony Gross, Lynton Lamb and Ceri Richards, receiving tuition from Andrew Forge, Lucian Freud and Claude Rogers (1956-59). He then travelled in Europe with the assistance of an Abbey Minor Travelling Scholarship, receiving in the same year (1959) a French Government Scholarship. Periods of teaching in Britain followed throughout the 1960s at Leicester College of Art, Nottingham College of Art, the Slade School of Fine Art, London, Coventry College of Art and Foley College of Art, Stourbridge. From 1970 to 1973 Sandle lived in Canada, where he was made Visiting Associate Professor at the University of Calgary, Alberta, until 1971 and then held a similar post at the University of British Colombia (1971-72).

In 1973 Sandle moved to Germany. Since 1980 he has held the post of Professor of Sculpture at the Akademie der Bildenden Kunste, Karlsruhe, the intervening years having been spent teaching in Pforzheim and as the guest of the DAAD artists programme in Berlin (1974-75). He was a member of the faculty of engraving at the British School in Rome (1976-82). He currently lives and works in Karlsruhe.

Michael Sandle has exhibited widely and has undertaken many commissions, the most significant being the *Memorial for the Victims* of a *Helicopter Disaster, Mannheim 1985*, his only major stone carving to date; *A Woman for Heidelberg 1987*, for a Heidelberg hospital; *St George and the Dragon 1987-88*, for the Mountleigh Group plc, in the City of London; *St Margaret 1991*, for the Pearl Assurance; and perhaps his most ambitious project to date, the Architecture and

Sculpture for the Malta Siege Memorial 1989-93, a vast commission which included not only a major figurative sculpture, but also a 13- tonne bronze bell.

Themes of war, death, destruction, inhumanity and media manipulation have been constant in Sandle's work. He treads a path outside the fashionable mainstream, choosing to explore difficult subject-matter whilst extending the use of traditional bronze casting and fabrication. Pushing forward possibilities in the use of materials was seen in *Crocus* 1963 and *Oranges and Lemons* 1966, both made in fibreglass-reinforced polyester, a medium he used for about fifteen years.

Sandle places great importance on refining technical skills and ideas. This passion is evident in his sculpture and drawing. Drawing is integral to his work, both as a means to develop ideas for sculpture and to create works of art in their own right.

Sandle was created Royal Academician in 1989 and Fellow of the Royal Society of British Sculptors in 1994.

William Turnbull

William Turnbull was born in Dundee, Scotland, in 1922. He worked as an illustrator in Dundee (1939-41) and studied at the Slade School of Fine Art, London (1946-48). For the next two years he lived in Paris, and on returning to London he became Visiting Artist at the Central School of Arts and Crafts (1953-61). He later taught sculpture there (1964-72) and now lives and works in London.

Both painter and sculptor, Turnbull finds sources for his work in other cultures and in classicism. A Chinese mask, the gateway to a Japanese Shinto temple, a primitive artifact from the tribes of Borneo or a small Cycladic goddess might be the starting point, or indeed a final reference. Abstraction is also important to Turnbull, and the issue of the marriage between abstraction and a desire to convey information in sculpture with great economy of form and precise content. Richard Morphet, in a catalogue to the exhibition *Sculpture in the Close* at Jesus College, Cambridge, in 1990, sums up his work: 'Turnbull's sculptures are intensely factual and their spirit is classical. Yet in their combination of formal concentration with runic articulation and metamorphic content they have a presence which approaches the magical.'

Turnbull has exhibited widely in Britain and abroad throughout his long career. His work is in public collections throughout the world.

Glynn Williams

Glynn Williams was born in Shrewsbury in 1939. He studied at Wolverhampton College of Art (1955-61). On graduating he won a Rome Scholarship for sculpture, and until 1963 lived and worked at the British School in Rome. After his return to England he taught at a number of art colleges including Leeds. In 1976 he was appointed to run the Sculpture Department at Wimbledon School of Art, setting himself the objective of building a department with clear aims and attitudes towards sculpture.

His first solo exhibition was held at the ICA in London in 1967, since when he has exhibited regularly in Britain and occasionally abroad.

Williams is a leading sculptor of the figurative tradition. Strong and solid forms based on the human figure, sliced and altered, have recently taken over from his more naturalistic sculpture. Some have been coloured or treated in ways that render surfaces more ambiguous.

Glynn Williams is currently Professor of Sculpture at the Royal College of Art, London.

Avril Wilson

Avril Wilson was born in Belfast in 1962. She studied at Ulster Polytechnic (1980-81) and gained a BA (1st class Hons) in three-dimensional design at Brighton Polytechnic in 1984. She was awarded an MA in ceramics at South Glamorgan Institute of Higher Education in 1985.

Since graduating, Avril Wilson has taught on a part-time basis whilst at the same time developing her own work as a blacksmith and sculptor. Her work reveals an interest in natural geometry, alchemy, medieval symbolism, mythology and organic form, all of which inform the aesthetic judgements she makes throughout her working process.

She has exhibited regularly in galleries, gardens and even a disused hardware store and a cemetery along the Brighton promenade. Frequently working to commission, Wilson enjoys the challenge of ensuring that the piece is relevant and appropriate to its surrounding environment. Recent commissions include forged steel spandrels in Banbury town centre (1993) and gates at The Hawthorns, Southampton (1995).

Avril Wilson lives in Brighton and is a member of Red Herring Studios.

Bill Woodrow

Bill Woodrow was born in Henley-on-Thames in 1948. He studied at Winchester College of Art (1967-68), St Martin's School of Art, London (1968-71) and Chelsea School of Art, London (1971-72). On graduating he showed work in a mixed exhibition at the Museum of Modern Art in Oxford and had his first one-man show at the Whitechapel Art Gallery, London, in 1972. There followed a period of around seven years when circumstances dictated that Woodrow made very little sculpture - he taught at an Inner London comprehensive school, and then full-time on a foundation course in Essex up to 1980. He would make work occasionally, but when in 1978 he got a studio he began to make sculpture on a regular basis.

Woodrow's early sculpture was made from materials found in dumps, used car lots and scrap yards, whether he was working in Britain or abroad. Large, disused consumer goods were the vehicle for his ideas - fridges, motorcar parts, doors, bricks and armchairs altered and placed in new relationships, formed metaphors for all kinds of tales. His 'archaeological' delving into modern detritus and the consequent narrative that he makes is aptly summed up in an essay by William Feaver (*The British Show* catalogue, Art Gallery of New South Wales/The British Council, 1985): 'Ransacking the debris of present-day civilisation, Bill Woodrow fabricates comparable apparitions. His sculpture is proverbial, fabulous. Cherishing the outlandish, rejoicing in the jump cut and the shock decision, he makes dry bones live.'

Collecting as he did, and using all manner of unrelated objects in new configurations, allowed Bill Woodrow to tell stories in his sculpture, and when he began to fabricate pieces in new material in the late 1980s, the narrative element remained. Recent works, cast in bronze, still evoke their eclectic origins, and the story told is equally elusive.

Acknowledgements

David Abramson

Clive Adams

Jane Allison

Robert Allison

Rosemary Baird

Nancy Balfour

Roger Bamber

Ian Barker

Pam Barnett

David Barrie

Marina Bauguil

Mary-Rose Beaumont

Monty Berman

Roger Berthoud

Roger Bevan

BOC

Erica Bolton

Anna Bowman

Sir Alan Bowness

Ivor Braka

Douglas Briggs

Sir Anthony Caro

Mark & Dana Cass

Eric & Jean Cass

Eva Chadwick

Chichester Institute

Cocking Quarry

David Cohen

David Coke

Caroline Collier

Dr Judith Collins

Chris Cooper

Richard Cork

Yvonne Connolly

Bronny Cunningham

Patrick Cunningham

Victor de Circasia

John Dewey

Zuleika Dobson

Miles Donnelly

Craig Downie

Nigel Draffan

Peter Eade

Jason Edwards

David Elliott

Biddy Elkins

Hilary Escolme

Nicholas Fisk

Angela Flowers

Julia Fogg

Christopher Fry

Patrick Gaynor

Paula Gibbs

R J Gibbs

John Gill

Anthony Goddard

John Godfrey

Lord Gordon Lennox

Lord Gowrie

David Gronow

Charles Hall

Geraldine Hamilton

Peter Harland

Derek Haworth

Gill Hedley

Angus and Anne Hewat

Michael Hewitt

Ros Hitchens

Robert Hopper

Michael Hue-Williams

Image Bank

Bernard Jacobson

Lin Jammett

Clare Jones

Annely Juda

Michael Kaufman

Jo Kelly

Rungwe Kingdon

Mervyn Kurlansky

Stephen Lacey

David Laker

Judy Lane

Gillian Lean

Jill & Stuart Le Fevre

Dr David Leigh

Sir Tom Lighton

Clare Lilley

Tim Llewellyn

Nicholas Logsdail

Susan Lopert

Annette Lovell

Prof Norbert Lynton

Elizabeth McCrae

Bill Malaclei

Earl of March

Tim Marlow

Meridian Fine Art

Peter Mimpress

Victoria Miro

Richard E Mitchell

David Mitchinson

Adrian Maokes

Marianne Moller

Catherine Morrish

Amanda Moses

Jim Moyes

Peter Murray OBE

National Trust, Mercia Region

Gerry & Anne Nutbeem

Paul O'Boyle

William Packer

Michael Peat

Susan Pratt

Jane Quinn

Duke of Richmond

Bryan Robertson

Steve Robson

Martin Russell

Paul Russell

Glenn Scott-Wright

Jo Seal

David Sekers

Nigel Semmens

Victor & Karen Shanley

James Shenton

Joe Smith

Roger Smith

Phil Stroud

Phillip Stroud OBE

Ann Sutton

Tate Gallery

Betty Thomson

Isobel Vasseur

Leslie Waddington

Richard Waite

Margaret Weld

Julia Whyard

Rob Widdows

David Williams

Bill Witcomb

Jonathan Witcomb

Marion Witcomb

Mark Wrey

Yorkshire Sculpture Park

Mary Yule

Copyright © 1996
The Hat Hill Sculpture Foundation

Texts
Ann Elliott

Editing
Angela Dyer

Design
Mervyn Kurlansky

Design Assistant
Marianne Moller

Photography
Judith Cox 75, Stan Dutton 61, Katsuhisa Kida 140
Sculpture at Goodwood 2, 15, 17, 19, 21, 23, 27, 29, 31, 33, 35, 37,
39, 41, 43, 45, 47, 49, 51, 53, 59, 65, 67, 71, 73, 77, 81, 85, 91,
93, 95, 97, 138, 139, 141, 142, 143, 144, 145, 146, 147, 148, 149
Richard Waite 25, 55, 57, 69, 79, 83, 87, 89, Don Wood 63

Printing
Crown Colourprint Limited

ISBN
0 9525233 1 0

Sculpture at Goodwood
Goodwood, West Sussex PO18 0QP
Telephone 01243 538449
Fax 01243 531853
Reg. charity no. 1015088

Open April - November
Thursday, Friday and Saturday 10.30 am - 4.30 pm